WHAT I WISH I'D KNOWN

for *Writers*

What I Wish I'd Known: For Writers

Copyright © 2023 by H. D. Thomson

Published by Bella Media Management

Book Cover by Bella Media Management

Printed in the United States of America for Worldwide Distribution

ISBN: Print Paperback – 979-8-9860460-2-0
ISBN: e-book – 978-1-7341515-9-6

WHAT I WISH I'D KNOWN
for *Writers*

100 authors reveal what they wish they'd
told their younger selves.

H. D. THOMSON

ACKNOWLEDGEMENTS

THIS BOOK WOULD NOT be possible without the time, energy, and knowledge of the authors who contributed. Several were in the middle of deadlines, while others scrambled to offer their thoughts when they were already juggling work, family, and just the plain craziness of life.

I would like to thank:

S.M. Anderson, Jennifer Ashley, Steven Barnes, Jeremy Bates, Louise Bay, D.V. Berkom, Hunter Blain, Marci Bolden, Rhys Bowen, Sarah Elizabeth Bromke, Benedict Brown, Rachelle Burk, V.M. Burns, Lynn Cahoon, Ginjer L Clarke, Nancy Coco, Michael Cordell, Charly Cox, B.J. Daniels, Vincent B. Davis II, Ernest Dempsey, Delaney Diamond, Helena Dixon, Angus Donald, Lorna Dounaeva, Kerrie Droban, Jacqueline Druga, Donna Everhart, Chris Fabry, Erin Flanagan, Matt Forbeck, Stacy Green, Ross Greenwood, Lisa Harris, Paul Heatley, Rita Herron, Kate Hewitt, Kelly Hodge, Dwight Holing, Griff Hosker, Daniel Hurst, Pamela Fagan Hutchins, Rick Jones, Diane Kelly, Meera Kothand, Justin Leslie, Julie Anne Lindsey/Bree Baker, Kristen Luciani, S.E. Lynes, JB Lynn, Michelle Major, Phillip Margolin, T. B. Markinson, Angela Marsons, Tina Martin, M.D. Massey, Cheyenne McCray, Cathy McDavid, Rhonda McKnight, Bruno Miller, J.J. Miller, Christopher Mitchell, Kiersten Modglin, D.J. Molles, Mary Monroe,

Lynn Morrison, Lisa Morton, Barbara Nickless, Nazri Noor, Peter O'Mahoney, Dan Padovan, Phaedra Patrick, Elizabeth Penney, Carly Phillips, Lisa Regan, David Ricciardi, Arianne Richmonde, Matthew Rief, Miranda Rijks, Dahlia Rose, Jenifer Ruff, Sofie Ryan, Sharon Sala, Pat Simmons, Joanna Campbell Slan, Miranda Smith, Jeff Strand, Jacquelin Thomas, Bill Thompson, Eric Thomson, H.D. Thomson, Michael J. Tougias, G.G. Vandagriff, Tim Waggoner, Dan Walsh, Rochelle B. Weinstein, Sherri Winston, D.L. Wood, Melinda Woodhall, and Pamela Samuels Young.

Thanks to Laurie Schnebly Campbell for your editorial advice. Your knowledge is invaluable.

I'd like to thank Kerrie Zhivago (Droban). As a great friend and fellow author, she's helped me through my writer's journey and getting through this thing called life.

It goes without saying that I would like to thank my husband, Tim Waltz. I would also like to stress how important hope and faith is not in just writing but in life. While putting together this book, Tim was battling metastatic melanoma. He struggled for over two years with cancer until he succumbed to the disease. If anyone deserved angel wings, it was him. He was my rock. Hearing stories from authors helped me tremendously during this dark time of my life and gave me faith when I needed it most.

CONTENTS

WRITE WHAT YOU LOVE OR WRITE FOR THE MARKET? 149

NETWORKING AND THE SOLITARY WRITER 169

HARD TRUTHS 179

INTRODUCTION

I NEVER USED TO like to read. While writing was something not in my vocabulary until I started college. It wasn't until I borrowed a book from my sister that my attitude toward books changed. She was a bookworm. Literally she would have her nose between the pages every spare moment she had. After several years, I concluded that there must be something great inside those covers for her to be so fixated.

Her fixation finally had me borrowing one of her books, and with that one act, I found myself falling in love. I quickly discovered reading was where I could escape, forget fear, problems, insecurities, and life's turmoil. I soon had favorite authors, favorite genres, and favorite books. When life was too much, I'd run to the library or bookstore and lose myself in words. Reading slowly inched into the idea of writing.

Everyone has a story inside them. It's up to that person if they want to tell it. The journey can be rigorous but at times remarkable, even magical. Within the pages of this book you will hear from 100 authors who tell their story, from craft, immense personal struggle, to hope, and frustration. You'll find differing opinions, but also there will be common themes. I hope those underlining themes will make you realize the more important factors that help you to become a successful writer.

I always thought writers were larger-than-life beings who magically conjured up stories. I had no idea what work was involved when it came to being an author and finishing a book. When I first started on this project, I didn't know what to expect. I didn't even know if I would be able find anyone willing to contribute. But it was the idea, not me, that had authors jumping on board and thrilled to add their story so they in turn could help others.

Some of these stories will move you, some will give you pause, but I hope they will help you on your writing journey. This book, I pray, will give its readers a chance to believe in themselves and their ability to help pursue their dreams of being a writer.

This book is not about becoming rich, monetarily, but becoming wealthy, and something far deeper than what money can buy. It's about pursuing a dream, becoming fulfilled, and enjoying the journey of becoming a writer.

Simply put, if you write, you are a writer.

WRITE

"Start writing, no matter what. The water does not flow until the faucet is turned on."

— Louis L'Amour

PAMELA FAGAN HUTCHINS

I'VE WRITTEN TWO DOZEN novels, filled reams of paper with business writing, and killed a forest with narrative nonfiction. I don't pretend I am a great writer. I'm becoming whatever writer it is I have the potential to be.

Fifteen years after first dipping my toe into fiction, I don't know whether I am a decent novelist or not. I do know this: I am fifty bajillion times better than when I started. And I won't fulfill my potential—however modest—unless I keep writing. I may write thirty novels before the potential gels. I dunno. I do know that if I stop, it will stagnate.

I have to write to be a writer.

Every time I sit down to write, I feel another piece of the puzzle fall into place. Maybe I finally understand how to rewrite my way out of a problem whose solution has eluded me for three years. Maybe I make my novel better. Tighter. Tenser. Faster. Let's say it's the best I have done so far. That it's the best I was capable of as of yesterday.

It is not the best I will ever do, or better than what I will write today.

Because three more books from now, I will have grown. Every

single time I feel like quitting because it's so *hard* and it isn't happening fast enough for me, I will have a cry and try again. On days when a story has me by the throat, I will rise at 3:00 a.m., make coffee, and write.

Practice makes perfect.

Here's the unvarnished truth: I have no idea on any day whether what I write will suck. I can edit it tomorrow and it may still suck. It may always suck. C'est la vie.

It will still be worth every second I invested in it. It will be forevermore a part of my becoming.

So, I will tilt my chin toward the sun and, just for today, I will believe. My work in progress may get published. It may not. But if nothing else, I will continue to write it, and the next "it," too.

Pamela Fagan Hutchins, *USA Today* bestselling author of crime fiction and Silver Falchion Best Mystery winner

PamelaFaganHutchins.com

LORNA DOUNAEVA

YOU DON'T HAVE TO *write every day.*

I used to write every day. I'd write first thing in the morning before work, on my lunch break, or late into the night. The words flowed and I enjoyed the creative process. Then I became a mum and my schedule had to change. I wrote when the baby napped or after he was down for the night, but I found it wasn't always possible to get the words in and I had to be okay with that.

Now I have three kids and writing is my full-time career. I know I'm capable of 12k a day, but I don't ask that of myself anymore.

It's not that I don't want to write – I absolutely do – it's just that I can't hit that flow state if I know I have to do the school run in an hour and I don't write well at night because I'm a morning person. If I want to get the words out it needs to be done early or I'll end up fighting myself. And that's not all:

The weekend is for my family.

I think it's healthy to take a break, so I try to keep weekends as family time. I also use this time to catch up on household tasks I might have let slip during the week. So I only write on the weekend if I'm really up against it. Most of the time, I shut my laptop down on Friday and that's it until the following Monday.

Life is too unpredictable.

Writing every day has never worked for me as a mother of three young children. You can't plan for when your children will be off with chicken pox, or when you'll be kept up all night because someone's come down with the flu.

Don't get me wrong, I'm the kind of person who loves to plan, and I like to know the future so I can control it. But if I try to plan months ahead it doesn't work for me. I have to flexi-plan. I have a general idea how long a book should take, but I can't accurately map out my time for more than a few weeks ahead.

A writer's work is more than the actual writing.

Whilst I'm always working on one book or another, I'm not always writing. I work in stages. I start with the premise. Then I play with different scenarios, different endings. I make a chapter list and get to know the characters. I do my research. This stage can last a few weeks.

Then I start the first draft and that's when I really throw myself into it. I love this part. It's intense, all-consuming so I work as many hours as my hectic homelife allows. And when I'm not writing, I'm thinking about it on the school run and in the park, or while I'm standing in the queue at the corner shop. During this stage, I often get up at the crack of dawn or stay up late so I can be fully emersed in the story. I live and breathe it. It's all I think about.

Then I come up for air.

I edit my novel and fall back down to earth. I rub my tired eyes and enjoy an early night. I catch up with friends and family. I catch up on my reading. Then I start to think about the next book.

Sometimes I break my own rules.

So I don't write every day. Unless I'm in the grip of a first draft. There are other bits and bobs that do sometimes leak into my weekends. Like writing newsletters and answering emails. Little bits of admin here and there. I might spend a bit of time on these over the weekend if I've got a lot to do, but this isn't as taxing as the actual writing. I love this job, and I love being able to work around my kids' school hours, but I don't have to write every day.

I do what works for me.

Lorna Dounaeva has a Masters in European Studies and used to work at the Home Office before turning to crime fiction. She lives in Godalming, Surrey with her husband, three children and a crafty cat.

LornaDounaeva.com

MATTHEW RIEF

MY BLANKET PROFESSIONAL ADVICE is to find someone who has the level of success that you want to have in the field that you want to be in, and do what they do. So, with regards to writing, decide what genre and subgenre you want to write in. Find the most successful authors in that genre (bestselling books on Amazon are a good start) and do what they do. Devour their books. Study them. Highlight and make notes and dogear those pages like mad. I often find myself reading the same paragraphs again and again because I'm trying to get some of that magic to rub off on me. Some of that greatness.

While doing that, write. Every. Single. Day. As much as you can. And don't make excuses. When I was writing the first in what would become my first successful series, my life was so busy that the only hour I could carve out for writing was from 4 to 5 in the morning. And I cherished that hour. I treated every minute like it was sacred. And I never wasted it. So find a time and treat it with reverence. If you really want to be a writer, this is what it takes. You need to buckle down and treat it with the importance it deserves. This will be very hard, especially at first. You will likely toil for years and years in obscurity. You'll likely rack up tens of thousands of seemingly fruitless hours. You need to push through this phase. It's necessary to find out how bad you really want it, and to make you a better writer.

I repeat, write. Every. Single. Day. I can't stress this enough. Set a word count goal. Every day. And stick to it. Act like your life depends on it. Don't feel like writing? Write anyway. There are days when I'm so inspired I swear it feels like Shakespeare and company are swirling around me, bestowing their literary nectar, and that my fingers are the instruments of creative brilliance. Then there are days where every word is like pulling a nail from a piece of plywood using those same fingers. It's often a struggle and requires you to dig deep. But the thing I realized a while back, the real game changer, was that while editing, I couldn't tell those days apart. The words I'd written during divine literary inspiration and the days when I felt actual pain, were indistinguishable. That's when you realize the secret—the real power isn't inspiration or appeasing the muse or what have you. It's consistency. That's how greatness happens. One of my favorite quotes regarding creative production is by the famous painter Chuck Close, who said, "Inspiration is for amateurs. The rest of us just show up and get to work. All the best ideas come out of the process; they come out of the work itself."

While writing as much and as good as you can, always be on the lookout for the best teachers—the best teammates to bring into the mix. Editors are invaluable. You find a good one? Treat them like royalty. Listen and soak in everything they say. Grow. Progress. Improve. I think it all boils down to that last thing. Always improve.

In short, I believe the essence of all self-help advice can be summed up into two words: Positivity and Action. Stay positive and take action. Do something. Write. Every. Single. Day. For years and years. And always improve. For me, that's the name of the game. The secret sauce, if there is any. Cheers.

Matthew, author of the Florida Keys Adventures and the Jason Wake series

MatthewRief.com

ARIANNE RICHMONDE

THERE IS NO WAY to become a writer if you do not write.

There is no way to know if you can do it or not if you do not try.

If you have an idea, jot it down on a napkin or the back of an envelope and save it. One of my books was created from a dream. When I woke up, I wrote it down. Do not think you have to have the perfect plot or the perfect ending already decided in your head. Many famous authors are "pantsers", they fly by the seat of their pants. They don't know what their ending is, and that's okay. If you have an idea, however small, give it value. Let it breath and grow.

Write it down.

Do not let them tell you that you cannot be a published author or there "is no money in writing."

Do not let them smash your dreams before you've even begun.

If I had known that I'd have success as an indie author, I would have started a lot sooner.

The beauty of being a published author today is that there are no gatekeepers, or there are (in traditional publishing), but you can ignore them if you choose and carve your own way into the publishing industry. You do not need an agent. You do not have to pick through dozens of rejection letters from agents any more. You no longer have to print hundreds of books at a time and have them rot in your garage. There is print on demand publishing, and you can create just one book if you want! And making an e-book is not as difficult as you might imagine. There are so many free tutorials on YouTube. Reams of Facebook groups for authors, with published authors offering tips. There is Google, where you can educate yourself in so many different ways on book publishing as an indie author.

Today's reality is: You can become a published author for FREE. It costs nothing to upload your book on Amazon and the other retailers. And, if you are good at learning and with a flair for design, you can even create your own book cover.

Obviously, if you have a little to invest, all the better, especially when it comes to an eye-catching book cover. If you can afford an editor and proofreader, that's great. If not, find beta readers to read through your first and second drafts. But there is no excuse for not letting your dream become a reality. Not these days.

One thing I have learned along the way is that there really isn't such a thing as a "good" or "bad" book. I have read novels I have considered atrocious, but readers have adored them. Likewise, there are books that win the Booker prize that readers say are "boring" and "poorly written." There are all types of books for all types of readers so, as a writer, do not second guess yourself. Study your craft as much as you can. Attend writing courses, if you can. But most importantly, read, read, read.

Read different genres. Read "good" books and "bad" books. Read widely.

But get going! The only true way to be a writer is to write. There will always be someone with more talent than you, but that doesn't mean you don't have a story to tell.

There are so many people who want to trample on dreams. People who will tell you that things are not possible, that you need to be "approved" by some higher authority in order to become a writer.

Not true.

A writer is somebody who writes. There is no wrong way or right way. There are no rules. And, yes, you can earn your living as a writer, don't let them tell you that you can't.

Now, pick up your pen, or open your laptop, and turn up to the page.

Turning up to the page and following through to the end is the very first step.

Good luck!

Arianne Richmonde, *USA TODAY* and #1 Amazon bestselling author.

ArianneRichmonde.com

DANIEL HURST

WHAT I WISHED I'D told my younger self – "You'll be amazed how many other people share the same dream to tell stories, yet how few will genuinely pursue it as they get older."

Although I'd spent most of my youth and early adult life scribbling down stories, mulling over ideas and fantasising about writing full-time, I was in my thirties before I decided to pursue it properly. When I did, it took great work ethic, discipline and above all, perseverance. But when the magical day came that I was able to quit my day job and replace it with writing, I was a little worried about what my employers might say about my reason for leaving. I'd kept it quiet about wanting to be a writer, so I knew it would come as a shock to them. I was mainly worried that they would feel like I had misled them somehow and that they would be irritated for having employed somebody who never had genuine ambitions in that particular industry.

But that didn't happen. *Instead, it was quite the opposite.*

Upon handing in my resignation letter (still the best thing I've written to this day!), my manager, a man in his fifties, told me that he actually had ideas for his own book and asked if I could help him with it. Then several others in the office came forward to reveal their own dreams of writing. This pattern continued with various friends, family members and all sorts of other people I encountered once I let it be known to the world that I had not only wanted to write but that I had actually done something about it. But it also became clear that while they all had ambitions to write something, very few of them, if any, had actually taken the quite crucial step of sitting down and placing their fingers on the keyboard.

The experience taught me that you can be either one of two kinds of writer. You can be the kind who writes, finishes a book and then figures out a way to get it in front of a reader. Or you can be the kind who has some vague idea of writing a book but never actually gets around to doing it, forever resigned to just telling others about your 'idea' whenever the subject of writing or dream jobs crops up in conversation.

There is nothing special about me. I just decided what I wanted to do and had a go at doing it. Anybody reading this can do the same thing. Be the kind of writer who writes. That kind is rarer than you think. Then one day, when you quit your old job to go and do your new one, you'll be amazed how many other people tell you they wish they could do the same thing.

Daniel Hurst is the bestselling author of the UK #1 psychological thriller *The Passenger*, as well as several other titles that have amassed over 100 million Kindle Unlimited page reads.

DanielHurstBooks.com

HUNTER BLAIN

MY JOURNEY BEGINS A little differently. It was birthed from a profound loss and a promise made to Sir John Cook* who was my childhood bestest good friend and bromego until his untimely passing in 2014 at the age of 32.

John had always enjoyed my short stories, which was something considering he was the type of friend that would straight up tell you if it sucked, and had asked me to write a book about him as a vampire. I jokingly promised I would do just that, only to realize the weight of it after it was too late.

One day out of the blue, a few years after John had left me, I felt the undeniable urge to fulfil my promise, and opened up my laptop. I could fight the ethereal drive no more than a drowning man could hold his breath just a few seconds longer after breaking the water's surface. My fingers danced over the keyboard as the story unfolded before my eyes, bringing with it hearty laughs, face contorting winces, and a warm tear or two.

And you know what? It felt *good*. Not only to keep my promise made to my best friend and doppelgänger but to see him live once more as John Cook, the smart-ass vampire. As of this writing, the *Preternatural Chronicles* has been read by several tens of thousands of people, each keeping him alive in the theater of their minds, thus making him immortal. A promise kept with staggering results I could have never anticipated.

So what is my advice?

To you, the aspiring writer, I would clearly say this: *write*. Take whatever inspiration flows your way, and run with it. Whether it be from the loss of a loved one, the previously unknown relaxation brought on by retirement, or just because you damn well feel like it. Write. No excuses.

When I was a district manager for various corporations, I had two sayings that I used when training people. The first was the cringe-worthy adage, "Whether you think you can, or you think you can't, you're right!" I hate it because it sounds like a thing a corporate district manager would say, but that doesn't detract from the fact that it is true.

The second was one of my own creation. Whenever someone gave me reason after reason as to why they couldn't meet the low bar that was minimum standards, I would say, "Excuses are like bullets, and I'm Keanu Reeves." I would be doing the employee a disservice if I accepted their excuses; and I offer the same advice to you, future writer. *No excuses*. If it is important to you, you will do it.

Take the last two paragraphs, and understand that you, and only you, will stop the words from flowing onto the paper. If you say "I don't have time to write because of XYZ," then you will never finish that novel you've been working on for 20 years. But if you make it a priority, even just a few hours on the weekend, it will be done in the blink of an eye. Want proof?

My first book took me a year to write. I only worked on it a few hours every Saturday, averaging probably 1,500-2,000 words at a time. Some days it could be 10 words, and a week later 10,000. But on average, let's just go with the 1,500-2,000.

52 weeks in the year, which means 52 Saturdays. See where I'm going with this? My first book was around 86,000 words, and you can do the rest of the math.

What's my point?

Close your eyes (not yet!), and imagine the year, say, 2018. What happened in that *entire* year? 12 months. 52 weeks. 365 days. And some catchy song about the buttload of minutes. How quickly can you recall all the important things you did in that year? For me, using the speed of thought, it is nearly instantaneous. Some would say *in the blink of an eye*. Isn't time funny like that?

In 2018, I spent a year working on book 1 in my series; and, in 2022, all I can remember is that I *did* it. I didn't have any excuses as to why I *couldn't*, only the overwhelming need to keep my promise.

So that is my first bit of advice to you: throw away any BS excuses, and write.

I have plenty more suggestions to give, but I've noticed 99.9% of people who ask for my advice can't get past the first step. Plus the other steps aren't as dramatic as what I just mentioned, nor are they as important as *write*.

Simple, ain't it? So simple that 99 full humans, and 9/10ths of another, aren't able to do it. Why? Because they *think* they can't. Which is a shame because there are so many untold stories out there, just waiting to be released into the wild. Instead, the ideas are condemned to pace back and forth in the cage made from thick skulls, only able to share their goodness with the lone zookeeper that keeps them prisoner.

Insert a Sarah McLachlan song (you know the one)

For just a few hours every weekend, you can free an idea that has only known darkness and isolation.

Won't you free your story?

Hunter Blain, okayest selling author of the Preternatural Chronicles, Sol Saga, and Chronos Paradox

HunterBlain.com

STEVEN BARNES

I WAS TEACHING WRITING at UCLA, and noticed something. The most common complaint from the students was lack of time in their lives. Man, it came up again and again. Everything: work, play, family, rest, eating…EVERYTHING got in the way.

So one week, feeling very sneaky, before I started teaching I started talking about television shows. I talked about my favorite show, and what had happened that week, relating it to our writing lessons. The conversation zipped along, and we spoke of character, plot, theme, and other stuff, all related to our favorite shows. I did this until EVERYONE in the class was in on the conversation.

And then I dropped the bomb:

"Everyone in this class watched at least three hours of television last week. Everyone in this class. That means every single one of you had time to write. Now: let's look at the lies you tell yourself to keep yourself from your dreams."

They were embarrassed, angry, and startled…but the conversation that followed was the best, and most useful we'd ever had.

~

Why do we do that to ourselves? Why deny ourselves the success, love, aliveness we could have? Inevitably, the biggest block is NOT something outside of ourselves, it is something IN US. Man, I could go on and on about this, but the simple truth is that we are our own worst enemies. NO ONE could possibly sabotage ourselves as much as we sabotage ourselves.

Want to see it in action? REMOVE ALL LOGICAL OBSTACLES.

This is the power of "write one sentence a day," one of the keys to the Lifewriting system. If you use this as not just a productive tool but a diagnostic, the world is yours.

1. Commit to write one sentence a day on your project. EVERY DAY. Do whatever it takes to convince yourself that this is a positive, necessary thing. Commit to it for 30 days.

2. NO ONE doesn't have time to write a single sentence in a day. No one. If you don't do it, you have broken your promise to yourself. The problem is then NOT your work, your kids, your time. Your problem is that you cannot trust yourself to keep your word. Note that if you can't…then no one else should trust you, either. You are SCREWED. As harsh as this sounds, it is the beginning of truth, and truth is the doorway to wisdom.

3. Ask yourself: why? Why didn't you keep a promise so apparently simple? It will ALWAYS boil down to some internal beliefs, values conflicts, or emotional storms. Voices in your head.

4. If you are honest enough, you will identify the SAME emotional storms stopping you in other arenas of life. What keeps you from writing a sentence a day stops you from losing weight, managing money, or finding a healthy relationship — first with yourself, and then with a significant other.

5. Once you see how this same set of lies, this same confusion and lack of focus stops you EVERYWHERE you are stuck, you should be able to tap into real grief and pain.

6. If you also have a clear vision of what you intend to accomplish, you have a "fork in the road" — one route leading to pain, the other to pleasure. INCREASE THE PAIN. CLARIFY THE HAPPY VISION.

7. How will you know when you "hurt" enough about the negatives, and feel wonder and joy about your vision? WHEN YOU TAKE POSITIVE ACTION. When you DO that simple sentence a day.

8. Keep track: are you doing your sentence? Yes? No? If yes, GREAT! It will naturally expand to more sentences. We'll explain why another time. If not... start the loop over again. What is stopping you NOW?

9. Continue this process until you can rely upon yourself to write that single sentence. Every day. Day after day. That's the key, you know: not "genius" except the

capacity to discipline yourself day after day to take another step along the Thousand Mile Road.

NY Times Bestselling author Steven Barnes has published over three million words of fiction, including science fiction, fantasy, horror, mystery, and historical. Winner of the Endeavor and NAACP Image Awards, nominated for Hugo and Nebula awards, he also writes film and television, his work appearing on STARGATE SG-1, ANDROMEDA, OUTER LIMITS, TWILIGHT ZONE among others. He lives in Southern California with his son Jason, and his wife and writing partner, American Book Award and British Fantasy Award winning author Tananarive Due.

Steven-Barnes.com

TINA MARTIN

I COME FROM A small town and was never really told to dream big. The only aspiration I had was to get a steady job. That's it. For me that ended up being something related to computers and accounting. The idea of being an author was absurd. Even to this day when I tell people I'm a writer, they don't believe it, or automatically assume you can't have a job that you're passionate about and still be able to make a living. That's simply not true and I wish someone would've told me that years go because I would've started writing a lot sooner. My writing career didn't take off until my mid-thirties. I remember feeling awful sitting at work, glued to a cubicle with no flexibility, always having to ask my manager if I can do this or that. On one occasion, I caught myself staring out the window on a bright sunny day asking myself why I couldn't be outside. I was stuck. Writing freed me.

I wish I'd known that while writing was my way out of that cubicle, it wouldn't guarantee overnight success. When I wrote my first book, I had dreams of making it big, but I didn't. I only had a handful of readers, but that didn't deter me because I'm a creator. I didn't give up because I love writing. It's like trying to lose weight – you work out for one week, didn't lose a pound, so now you stop trying?? No. We don't stop trying. We keep going and get better.

The best advice I can give writers is, if you want to be a writer, you must write. When I had a corporate job, I wrote when I got off work. I wrote on my lunch breaks. I wrote sitting in doctor offices, waiting to be called back for an appointment. I wrote in the drive thru. I wrote whenever I got the chance to write. I knew I had a gift for it, even though I wasn't trained in it and eventually, the words flowed faster and the ideas were plentiful. I turned something I loved into my career. You can't call yourself a writer if you don't write, so try to do it everyday even if it's just a few sentences.

Tina Martin, award-winning *USA Today* bestselling author who has written over 80 titles.

TinaMartin.net

V.M. BURNS

FOR YEARS, I TOLD myself that one day, I would become a writer. When? I would become a writer…after I hit the lottery, quit my day job, the planets aligned perfect, etc. After all of those things, then and only then could I BECOME a writer. If I could go back in time, I'd tell my younger self, to write. Writers don't sit around dreaming about writing. Writers write. I argued that I didn't have time. I was busy. One day, I realized that I had the same twenty-four hours in my day that everyone else had. If I wanted to be a writer. I had to stop dreaming and *just do it.* If something is important, you make time for it. If writing was important, then I had to MAKE time for it. Eventually, I got the revelation, and that's what I did. I'm not an early morning person. I'd heard about several successful writers, like James Patterson, who wrote early in the morning. I am not a morning person. I am not going to get up at 4, 5, or even 6am to do anything. Besides, anything I wrote at that time of the day wouldn't be appropriate for human eyes. Instead, I looked at my day and everything that I had to do and found my ideal time. For me, the best time for writing was in the evening. So, that's what I did. I wrote from 10-12pm every night. When I was on a roll, sometimes, I went later. On bonus days, I squeezed in a writing session during my lunch hour on the day job. I've learned to keep a small notepad and pen in my car and in my purse. So, I can write in the waiting room at the doctor's office, in the lounge while getting my oil changed, or while stuck in traffic. Somedays those bonus sessions may only add a few words to the daily word count, but every one of those words add up in the end. After a few weeks, writing becomes a habit. If you want to be a writer, then my advice is to figure out what day/time fits into your life as it exists right now and write. Before you know it, those late night/early morning writing sessions will result in a finished manuscript. And you'll have become the writer you dreamed you could be.

V.M. Burnes is an AGATHA AWARD-NOMINATED author of the Mystery Bookshop series and the short story, The Vermeer Conspiracy, and also a NEXT GENERATION INDIE BOOK FINALIST. V.M. is the author of the RJ Franklin Mystery, Dog Club Mystery, Baker Street Mystery, and Pet Detective (Coming 2023) series. She works as an adjunct professor in the Writing Popular Fiction Program at Seton Hill University in Greensburg, PA

Bookbub: https://www.bookbub.com/authors/v-m-burns
Facebook: https://www.facebook.com/vmburnsbooks/
Instagram: https://www.instagram.com/vmburnsbooks/
Twitter: https://twitter.com/vmburns
VMBurnes.com

BRUNO MILLER

WRITING POST-APOCALYPTIC FICTION is probably the last thing I would have guessed I'd be doing five years ago. In fact, writing wasn't even on my radar. If it wasn't for my sister's encouragement, also a writer, I most likely would not be making a living today telling stories.

If I had to give aspiring authors any words of wisdom it would be this. Push through the self-doubt and write the book. There are many books out there for aspiring authors, each with their own methods and suggestions describing how to get your words onto paper. A personal favorite of mine is Steven King's, *On Writing*. The Pomodoro Technique, the mini-goal technique, the Snowflake Method, the jigsaw method... There are many more, and a quick Google search will yield endless results.

The countless different approaches to writing are enough to make your head spin and I think ultimately can discourage you from ever starting your novel. And while these methods may work for some, I believe the most important thing a writer can do is find a routine and commit to it. That may include plotting an outline with an ending in mind or just winging it. But regardless of the method, writing requires commitment. There's that word again.

Writing is a creative process and, in my opinion, it's counter-productive to put parameters on creativity. Where I believe a prospective writer can be stringent is in setting aside a dedicated time to disconnect from the world and tell your story.

Many authors set daily word goals and while I do this myself, beware the pitfalls of word goals. I know of successful authors who shoot for 500 words a day, and others that aim well into the thousands. Be careful not to set yourself up for failure with unrealistic expectations. 3000 words a day is an outstanding accomplishment unless you spend the following day rewriting most of it.

You're going to have bad days. Nearly five years in and there are times when I push away from the monitor and wonder what in the world it is that I think I'm doing. I've heard it called imposter syndrome and a few other things, but self-doubt in any form can wreck your productivity and creative flow. Some of my best days writing have had less than stellar beginnings. Get up, go for a walk outside, play with the dogs, get another cup of coffee, and then come back and try again.

Find what works for you and get writing.

Amazon best-selling author Bruno Miller is the author of the Dark Waters, Dark Road, and Cloverdale series. He's a military vet who enjoys spending his downtime with his wife and kids, or getting in some range time. He believes in being prepared for any situation.

BrunoMillerAuthor.com

HELENA DIXON

WHAT I WISH I'D known as a new writer is that time spent not writing can be as important as time spent writing. Time spent reading, taking a workshop, talking to other writers, learning about the industry is equally as valuable. Time spent planning or thinking about your story before you set words down on the page. Time experiencing life or travelling. Time researching is all part of the process.

That's not to say that you don't have to write. At the end of the day, you can't be a writer unless you're writing, but all of the other things I've mentioned can make what you write something someone else wants to publish, buy or read.

Helena Dixon – Multi award winning author of the best-selling Miss Underhay series.

NellDixon.com

S.M. ANDERSON

LIKE MOST ASPIRING WRITERS who are considering writing a story for self-publication or to shop around to the traditional publishers, I spent years reading and listening to everything I could on the how tos. How to write, how to edit, how to find an agent, how to market, the list is endless. I knew I wanted to write. In my heart, I knew I was a writer. What I didn't appreciate was the level of commitment and work it takes to make that a reality. I wish I could go back twenty years and have a talk with my younger self.

Looking back, I realize all I really needed to take on board from my research was a small list of nuggets. The most important has been said and paraphrased a thousand different ways. I personally like - "put your ass in the chair and write every day." It sounds easy. It sounds like a no brainer. For me, it was and continues to be the most difficult aspect of writing. But that simple truism isn't enough. For me, what you write everyday was the missing piece.

Which brings me to idea two; and it's one I'm taking credit for because it's made all the difference for me personally. "Shoot the good idea fairy – in the head." Ok, that sounds harsh I know. But remember, this is advice to my younger self. The younger me would understand you need to listen to the idea fairy, write down whatever he/she says for later consideration – then shoot. It's my conceptual image of saying you need to finish the project you are working on. Pick a project and write it to completion. Distractions are always there, and none of them are as powerful or as alluring to me as a new idea. I could have spent another decade or the rest of my life writing every day jumping from one story to the next. I wouldn't have had anything to show for it beyond another several dozen story starts for which I lost all enthusiasm for, the minute the idea fairy started buzzing around my head. The first 20K words of a story are always easy. Daily work is important, but it is *focused* daily work that produces something that can be edited, made better, given a cover, marketed, and read.

Finishing something to completion forced me to look at a story as a whole – see where it falls down, where it slows, where it loses coherence, or goes off theme. You can write every day jumping from one idea to the next and you *will* get better at building characters, creating worlds, or writing believable dialogue. None of that will necessarily make you a better story teller. Stories have an ending, and you need practice getting there.

One of the most surprising things about my writing life is the number of young writers that write me for advice. A lot of them seem to be in love with *the idea* of being a writer. I don't know why. There are a million different ways to make a living that are more profitable, and less demanding. I always ask them; do you love writing? Not on weekends when you have some free time with a beer or beverage of your choice, but every day, for hours in the morning before you go to work or at night after everyone else has gone to bed? If you don't love the act of writing that much, save yourself the frustration and make the decision to write for fun, when it's easy, when you feel like it.

In my opinion, that's what it takes. Put your ass in the chair and work on a project to completion every day. If you can get beyond the idea of wanting to be a writer and internalize the habit of producing something on a daily basis, you're there. Well, you're halfway there, because this is a business...

Marketing and selling your product is a world away from the skill set needed to create it. You have to be able to take your writer's hat off, gauge your product objectively from a market sense, and move out with a plan to put it front of readers. Readers are going to be the ultimate arbiter of success. Doesn't matter if you think someone else's best-selling book is a talentless, vapid portrayal of an over done Hollywood trope. At some level, it has sold, and for hundreds of thousands if not millions of readers it filled a need or an interest.

You are never going to know how this is done. If you did, it would be valid for six months. People's tastes, needs, trends change constantly. It's just my opinion, and should be taken as such - but don't chase anything. Write a story that excites you. If you can't maintain the enthusiasm for writing a story for the six months, year, or seven years that it took me to finish my first book - readers probably won't get excited about it either.

Finally, if you do fall down this rabbit hole and decide on a writing life. Understand, the writing advice never ends. I think all of it is well-meaning, and absolutely valid for the people giving it. That does not make it right for you, and that includes everything I've written here. A lot of the advice will focus on how to produce enough work to make writing a valid career choice. In my very humble and admittedly still forming opinion – I can only say be true to yourself and use what works for you. For example, I'm a "panster" - I don't outline. I get a story idea, a concept of how it ends, characters and a setting in mind. Then I start writing and figure out how to have fun getting to 'The End.'

The only writer's block I've ever had is when I gave outlining a serious effort. I read the right books, I listened to the right podcasts. I sat for weeks trying to outline a novel in advance with nothing to show for it. Worse still, my imaginary gun ran out of ammo and I didn't have a current work in progress to keep the idea fairy at bay. Is outlining bad? No. I'm intellectually honest enough to know that having an outline conveys a significant advantage in terms of output. I'm jealous as hell of those writers who can outline and then write an enjoyable, entertaining story. It just doesn't work for me. It took some time for me to accept that. Try new things, maybe you can go for a walk and dictate your story. I can't. Whatever you figure out regarding your process, commit to it, and put in the work.

S.M. Anderson is a former CIA Operations Officer and an Amazon best-selling author with two series published. He lives in Virginia with his wonderfully supportive family and writes in his basement where no one can hear the idea fairy screaming. His post-apocalyptic series "Seasons of Man" will wrap with the soon to be released book three. His military/sci-fi series "The Eden Chronicles" has four books out currently, with much more planned.

SMAnderson-Author.com

CRAFT

"You don't start out writing good stuff. You start out writing crap and thinking it's good stuff, and then gradually you get better at it."

— Octavia E. Butler

KELLY HODGE

MY BACKGROUND, LIKE MANY writers who have suddenly had to reinvent themselves, was in the newspaper business. I spent three decades working for my hometown paper, following in my father's footsteps right out of college, before the industry began to collapse. Right at the top of the list of "What I Wish I'd Known" was how quickly that collapse would play out.

Making the transition from sports journalism to commercial fiction, at 55, was an immediate and daunting challenge. I found there to be little in common between the two, other than the daily demand for imagination and discipline.

Deadlines drive everything in the newspaper business; you're always watching the clock, trying to gauge how much time you can afford the story of the moment. The copy can be cringe worthy when you see it in print the next day, but that's the nature of the beast and you live with it.

As an independent author, deadlines are self-imposed and often arbitrary. There is time to ponder the storylines — and ponder, and ponder, and ponder. That's where the discipline comes in. You have time to work your magic, but don't waste it. Get on with the story. The first inclinations are typically the best, and you have to trust yourself. Just keep things moving; readers will appreciate it.

I was fortunate to have a bestselling author in the family. Scott Pratt was my brother-in-law, a friend, a mentor and, at last check, a man who has sold more than four million books. He was also a newspaper guy in a former life, and a passionate observer of sports. We wrote and thought a lot alike. When I wondered if I could make the transition to crafting novels, and how to go about it, I had to look no further than Scott for counsel and encouragement.

Scott has been gone for three years now, having lost consciousness on a scuba diving excursion off the coast of Bonaire, in the southern Caribbean. But his memory is very much alive in his many works, including our collaboration on the first three Billy Beckett books. (The fourth, *Break Point*, was released in October.)

Perhaps the most valuable insight Scott offered to an aspiring writer of fiction was this: You need a good story, but you need *great* characters. Readers will follow interesting, compelling characters wherever the story takes them. That's still the driving thought as I sit down at the keyboard every morning.

Kelly Hodge, creator of the Billy Beckett adventure crime novels.

KellyHodge.Squarespace.com

LOUISE BAY

THE MAIN THING I wish I'd known when I first started out on my writing journey was that sometimes you have to write to get better. So stop revising that draft and just move on to the next project. I always tell people who are writing their first book to just get it done and move on to the second book which will be better.

I also wish I'd used a developmental editor earlier. I had an editor that thought she was but she was basically a copy editor and I didn't know better. Once I started working with a good developmental editor, my writing quickly got a lot better. I think she was secretly dismayed that I'd already hit USA Today before I started working with her. But I wouldn't have continued to hit it consistently without her help. First lesson? You gotta have conflict to get people to turn the page.

The best advice I ever got as a mother and the advice I now always pass on is that everything's a phase. I tell myself this all the time at three in the morning when my daughter has woken me up twice already. It's true of life too. Sometimes you just have to cling on until the eye of the storm passes. And then you have to make hay while the sun shines.

USA Today bestselling author, Louise Bay writes sexy, contemporary romance novels – the kind she likes to read.

LouiseBay.com

39

MICHAEL CORDELL

WHEN I FIRST BEGAN writing, whenever I was fleshing out my initial story idea and encountered a question I had to answer, I often went with the first solution that came to mind. For example, let's say I was writing a screenplay (although the same thing applies to writing novels), about a young woman (18-ish years old) who lives on a ranch, and who is attracted to a young man who had just started working there, and I needed a scene that showed she was drawn to him.

My initial impulse might be to have the young man walk into the room and the young woman would get nervous and knock over a glass of water and become flustered. Or the young man might ask her a question and she would become so nervous she'd start to stammer or say something embarrassing.

But the reason I first thought of the scenario where she spills something due to nerves is because I have probably seen that a million times before. And the stuttering out of nervousness is something I've seen half a million times.

Often times, the first solutions we come up with to story questions come to mind quickly because they are things we have seen in scores of other stories. This recognition led to me to start trying, wherever possible, to adopt the _Rule of Ten._

Now whenever I come across a story decision I need to make, I try coming up with ten possible solutions. As would be expected, the first few solutions are the usual cliches, but by the time I reach option seven or eight, I've started moving toward something more original.

It's not always easy coming up with several different solutions to a story problem, but that's a good thing. The Hollywood reader, who is charge of finding a great script—or the literary agent looking for a great manuscript—reads hundreds, if not thousands, of stories and, therefore, they are usually able to see what's coming in a story a mile away.

It's hard to surprise these people, because all they do is read screen-plays/manuscripts. So if the writer him/herself has to spend a considerable amount of time coming up with original approaches to their story's various questions, the chances are great the reader won't immediately think of them, which means the reader will be surprised, which means the reader will be happy, which bodes well for your submission.

This is the same reason why painting yourself into a corner when writing your story can be a great thing, although it usually doesn't feel like it at the time. When you come to a point in your story where even you, *the writer*, don't know how you're going to get your protagonist out of the situation you've put them in, and it takes you days, weeks, or even months to figure out the solution, then you can be assured the Hollywood or literary reader won't be able to figure it out during their read. Not knowing what's going to happen next—and wanting to know what's going to happen next—is the killer combination I want my readers to experience when reading my stories.

This often isn't easy, but then again, great storytelling probably shouldn't be easy.

So be suspicious anytime a solution to a story question comes too quickly or easily. Get in the habit of identifying several different ways in which you can address your story's questions, and remember that the harder it is to think of those solutions, the stronger your story is likely going to be.

By the way, the scenario I mentioned at the beginning was a scene from the 1982 movie "The Man From Snowy River." In this film, the screenwriter was faced with having to convey the woman's attraction to the young man, so he set the scene with the woman practicing a well-known classical piece of music on the piano, with her mother sitting next to her on the piano bench, giving her instructions. She was playing it fine, albeit it a bit mechanically and uninspired. The young man entered the room and talked with the two women for a couple of minutes and then, after he left, the young woman started playing the song again, but this time she played it with such emotion and tenderness. Even her mother looked over at her, quizzically, as if trying to figure out what was going on. We could all but hear the love she felt in those notes.

It was such a wonderful way to reveal her feelings toward this young man, and to do it in a way that allowed her to be an intelligent, three-dimensional person (instead of someone bumbling when nervous), and it enabled us to see into her heart without her having to say a word or having her do anything obvious. I'm guessing this approach was on the screenwriter's list of ten options, because it was subtle, it was original, and it was beautifully memorable.

All of our writing should aspire to that.

Michael Cordell is a novelist, playwright, and produced screenwriter. His screenplay "Beeper" is an action-thriller starring Harvey Keitel, and his novel *Contempt* was an Amazon top ten legal thriller. Michael's paranormal suspense novel *Our Trespasses* won the Silver Falchion award for mystery writing.

MichaelJCordell.com

PETER O'MAHONEY

I LOVE WRITING. I love taking the audience on a journey of emotional ups and downs, mysterious twists and turns, and ending with explosive surprises. While I love the process of writing a novel, I'm also on a journey of continual improvement.

At this point, I've written 16 novels, including a number of legal thrillers, and I plan to write many more. Writing novels isn't about luck, or some inherent skill we have inside us, it's about hard work and improvement.

On my journey, I've learned that there are three distinct skillsets involved in writing a novel. If you're like me and want to improve as an author, it's important to acknowledge that becoming a better writer involves improving all three skillsets.

These three skillsets are:

- The Art of Storytelling;
- The Art of the Prose; and
- The Art of Editing.

The Art of Storytelling

As the name suggests, this is the art of writing an engaging story that hooks the reader and ensures they keep turning pages. It doesn't matter if you're writing thrillers, romance, sci-fi, or literary fiction, engaging the reader in the story is essential.

At the center of any great story is interesting characters. They have to be fascinating, on one level or another, and the reader has to want our heroes to succeed and our villains to fail (or our characters to be confused about where the line of good and evil is drawn). There has to be a reason that drives the character to do what they do.

Other than interesting characters, the reader becomes engaged in the novel by giving the story a destination. For example, in a legal thriller, the defense lawyer wants to get the client off the charges. In a mystery, the hero wants to solve the puzzle. In a romance, the main character wants to fall in love.

Suspense is then created by adding obstacles as the characters work towards their desired outcome.

My Process for Storytelling

I spend weeks planning a story before I even write a word. I'll sit with another author, sometimes over lunch or other times over a whiskey, and talk about ideas for the story. We'll write out ideas and work with each other to create something engaging for the reader.

Once that is done, I'll sit in my office with a whiteboard and map out the three acts of the novel.

The first act is usually a quarter of the novel and is the set-up of the story. This act starts with a hook and ends with a hook. The second act is usually two-quarters of the novel, and this is the main part of the story. This is where the investigation takes place, with a few ups and downs along the way. And the last act is the last quarter of the novel. This is where everything comes together, and it's action, action, action.

Once the three acts are planned, I'll write out a chapter outline. This outline is usually 50-200 words per chapter and details what, where, and how things will happen.

It's important that each chapter moves the story forward, and has interesting information for the reader. I try to end 80% of chapters with a hook, which ensures the reader doesn't want to put the novel down.

During this process, I also refine the characters, ensuring they're all interesting in one way or another, and the reader wants to know more about them.

Once all this is done, it takes me to the next stage of writing:

The Art of the Prose

This is the art required to write a great sentence, a great paragraph, and a great page.

This is different for every genre, and it's important to understand your audience. The prose in a literary fiction novel is different from the prose of a thriller, and the prose of a thriller is different from the prose of a romance novel. If you look at the top sellers of any genre, they tend to have the same writing styles.

What all writers must have, regardless of genre, is rhythm. The best quote about rhythm in writing is from author Gary Provost, and I often refer to this quote when writing:

This sentence has five words. Here are five more words. Five-word sentences are fine. But several together become monotonous. Listen to what is happening. The writing is getting boring. The sound of it drones. It's like a stuck record. The ear demands some variety. Now listen. I vary the sentence length, and I create music. Music. The writing sings. It has a pleasant rhythm, a lilt, a harmony. I use short sentences. And I use sentences of medium length. And sometimes, when I am certain the reader is rested, I will engage him with a sentence of considerable length, a sentence that burns with energy and builds with all the impetus of a crescendo, the roll of the drums, the crash of the cymbals—sounds that say listen to this, it is important. — *Gary Provost.*

The Art of Editing

This is the art of looking at your work subjectively.

Sometimes, this is hard because we're all so deep into a story and, as authors, we become attached to certain parts. But the key to this art is stepping back and looking at the piece as a whole—where does it lack and where can it be improved. Obviously, editors are employed to do this (and I have an awesome team behind me), but an author must also be able to do some parts of this themselves.

I'm a big fan of the 'bottom-drawer' approach. When I've

finished a story, I put it away for weeks and try not to think about it. I'll move onto the next book, and wipe my memory clean of the last one. After a while, I'll return to the last manuscript and re-read it with fresh eyes. During this process, I realize that some clues are too obvious, and some aren't obvious enough. I notice that some characters are too boring, and others have too much happening. I realize that some chapters aren't needed, or others need to be moved to later in the book. And I'll notice that some of the writing is just plain tedious and needs to be improved.

It's during this process that the manuscript is refined and tightened. After I've self-edited, I'll send it onto my editor, who'll do the same thing. Often, the last draft is very different to the one I put in the bottom drawer only weeks earlier.

Everyone has different strengths and weaknesses, and different approaches to writing, but if there's one thing that all authors should do, it's praise each other when we've got it right. We all need a pat on the back every now and again.

If I've read a good book, I'll make sure to email the author to tell them that I love it.

Good luck on your writing journey.

Peter O'Mahoney, Criminologist and author of the Tex Hunter and Jack Valentine thrillers, with more than a million books sold worldwide.

PeterOMahoney.com

PAMELA SAMUELS YOUNG

WHEN I DECIDED TO write a legal thriller, that's exactly what I did. I sat down and started writing. At the time, I was a practicing lawyer, a former television news writer and an avid reader of all things thriller. How hard could it be? I spent the next three years writing a novel that I—and I alone— thought was a masterpiece. Only after repeated rejection from agents, did I ultimately find my path.

Here are three things I wish I'd known.

First, it's essential to master the writing craft. I had no trouble writing a persuasive legal brief or an enticing story for the six o'clock news. But I knew nothing about how to write a novel. I didn't fully understand point of view. I gave no thought to story structure. I had no clue about creating conflict, nor did I under-stand the importance of hooking a reader at the end of the chapter. When I say *master the writing craft*, I don't just mean take a few writing courses. That's key, of course, but you should also study authors in your genre whose work you admire and enjoy. Always, always, always read like a writer. Analyze why you enjoyed a book. Make a note of the things you liked as well as the aspects you didn't.

The most enlightening thing I did as an unpublished author was to outline a novel, something an instructor at a writing seminar suggested to the class. I chose the quintessential legal thriller, *The*

Firm by John Grisham. I outlined the book as I would a college paper. I summarized each chapter in a couple of sentences, then meticulously dissected the book. Was the pacing fast, slow or just right? Was there sufficient conflict? Were the twists unexpected? How did each chapter begin? Did every chapter end with an enticing hook?

Even today, years later, I can still remember the lightbulb moment that exercise sparked for me. I finally began to understand how to structure a compelling story. I soon found my voice and honed my signature, fast-paced writing style. I ended up shelving my first novel and applying everything I'd learned about the writing craft to a second effort. A year later, I'd completed the book, which attracted the interest of three agents. Within months of signing with an agent, I had a two-book publishing deal.

Second, don't fall in love with your writing to the point that you're unwilling to listen to constructive criticism. It's important to have a team of test readers whose opinion you respect—and not just other writers, but avid readers too. If they don't love your book, it's likely that the general public won't either. So don't be afraid to solicit feedback. Listen carefully to what your test readers like, what they don't like and what they don't understand. In the end, only make the changes you're comfortable with. But if five people you trust read your manuscript and all five tell you X doesn't work, it probably doesn't.

When I sat down to write my first novel, I foolishly expected to write a first draft that would be an instant bestseller. I soon learned that the real writing is in the rewriting. Rewriting is now the part of the writing process I enjoy most. There are times when I end a writing session thinking that I've crafted the most amazing prose ever. But when I reread it a day or two later, it doesn't seem that great at all. And I *always* find ways to improve it. So remain open to *constructive* criticism.

Third, ignore the naysayers. Many people dash other people's dreams because they're too afraid to pursue their own. When I proudly told anyone who would listen that I was working on a legal thriller, more than a few people warned me that it would be hard to get a book deal. They were right. It *was* hard, but it wasn't impossible. Don't let pessimistic people deter you from pursuing your goals. The publishing world is full of authors who were told they'd never make it. John Grisham, Steven King, J.K. Rowling, just to name a few. Yet, they all went on to publish books that sold millions.

If you master the writing craft, recognize the value of constructive criticism, and turn a blind eye to naysayers, you *will* reach your goal of becoming a published author.

Pamela Samuels Young, attorney and award-winning author of *Anybody's Daughter,* has written multiple legal thrillers. She is also on the board of directors of Sisters In Crime, Los Angeles, an organization dedicated to the advancement of women mystery writers.

PamelaSamuelsYoung.com

DAN WALSH

THINGS HAVE DRAMATICALLY CHANGED since my first novel was published in 2009. In my personal life, but even more so in the world of publishing. If someone traveled back in time to that moment and told me how things would be in 2022, I'd find it impossible to believe. Back then, traditional publishing was king.

There were no other viable alternatives. You either got an A-list agent to take you on and hope she (or he) grabbed the interests of a mainstream publisher, or you kept trying. Most of the published authors I met early on told tales of how challenging and difficult their "publishing journey" had been. Many had their work rejected dozens of times before someone said yes. Or had written numerous novels—all rejected—before their first one finally hit the shelves.

Through all those hard times, these authors would never have thought of "going indie." It just wasn't done. The only place people bought books back then was at traditional brick-and-mortar stores, and those stores would never accept books unless the publishing house was legit and well-known. Amazon did exist in 2009, but its economic impact was negligible.

When I received my first royalty statement, ebooks accounted for less than 3%. Fortunately for me, I did not have a harrowing publishing tale. I submitted my first novel (a Christmas book called *The Unfinished Gift*) to three A-list agents (the first three on my list) and two of them instantly got back with me, asking to read the entire book. I signed with one a week later, and eight weeks after that she had a contract with a major publishing house. It was on the shelves all over the country the following holiday season.

That novel released to raving reviews and wonderful sales. It won two major writing awards in 2010, and my writing career kinda took off. That year, my publisher was literally begging me to leave my full-time job to write full-time (and were willing to match my salary). I made the leap and spent the next five years under contract with them, writing a total of 13 novels.

It seemed to me like this would be my writing life forever. But that's not how the story ends.

Even by 2012, I was seeing this "Indie Invasion" emerging, mainly due to the rapid rise of Amazon and Kindle. That year they came out with a Kindle for $99 and sold millions of them. In one year, my ebook sales grew to almost 50% of my total sales. Then came the free Kindle app, available on any device. Then Amazon Prime, where print books would be delivered to your door in two days, no shipping fees.

And they were offering authors the opportunity to make 70% on their retail book sales (they would take 30%). No middleman gobbling up all your book earnings. That was at least five times what I was getting from my publishing contracts, per book sold. So, like many of my bestselling author friends, I made the leap to indie publishing.

It's been a great experience for me. My only regret is not doing it a couple of years sooner. I now have 27 novels out. About half of them are books my publisher wouldn't accept, because they were "not my brand." My sales and income now far exceed my best years in the traditional arena.

And with this Indie Revolution, literally, hundreds of new authors have been able to get their books published online. Authors who had only experienced rejection from traditional houses. The problem is—and I'd say it's a big one—so many of these new authors after a year or so, are NOT feeling very satisfied with their publishing experience, in terms of sales or growing a viable readership.

I often teach at writer's conferences, so I've looked into this issue pretty thoroughly. And I've come to this conclusion…which will also serve as my primary advice to new writers hoping to experience success in their writing careers.

Here's the reality of it. Regardless of the packaging or format, whether it be a print book or ebook, from a traditional publisher or an indie, from a brick-and-mortar store or one online…readers are all looking for the same thing.

Every reader wants to read a great story, well told.

That's it. If you can write it, they'll buy it, read it, and love it. They'll check to see if you've written any other books, and they'll tell their reader friends, "You gotta read this book."

That's what happened in my traditional writing years, and it's still happening now as an Indie. And I think the reason is…back then, if you didn't focus on THE CRAFT OF WRITING, you didn't get in the club. Even though it made for a tough road to travel, I think it forced writers to put all their attention where it should be… learning how to write a great book.

It's very easy to market a great book, almost impossible with a mediocre one. I think the Indie Revolution has flooded the market with mediocre books. That's not what readers want. Not what they have ever wanted. Just tons of available cheap books. They want books they can't stop reading once they start, with characters they're still thinking about days after they've finished.

So, that's my advice. Learn how to write great books. Do that, and there's a realistic chance you can still succeed in this brave new publishing world. Because that's what readers want, what I'm always looking for as a reader myself.

A great story, well told.

Dan Walsh is the bestselling author of 27 novels (all available on Amazon), including *The Unfinished Gift*, *Rescuing Finley*, *When Night Comes*, and *The Reunion* (soon to be a feature film). Over 1.2 million copies of Dan's books are in print or downloaded.

DanWalshBooks.com

D.J. MOLLES

WHAT DO I WISH I'd known as a younger author? Well, literally everything I've learned between 2012 and the moment you're reading this, whenever that is. The years have been chock full of new lessons. But that is a huge part of being a writer—continuously learning, experiencing, thinking, perceiving, talking, and listening. Learn voraciously. There are ideas hiding everywhere. You collect enough ideas, you can make stories out of them. But you have to be the one to reach out and grab them, which means you have to see them first, which means you have to be paying attention. I guess that's my first piece of advice. Some of the other big ones from my personal experiences over the last decade are...

I learned that writing is mostly a craft. The moments of "art" come when you are writing your rough draft with reckless abandon, and not giving two shits what it looks like, sounds like, or what anybody says—you're just putting black on white, you're putting your heart on the page, damn the consequences. That's art. But that's a small part of what we do. All the other stuff—outlining, world building, character building, plotting, editing, synopsizing, etc.—that's all craft. And craft is based on knowledge and practice. It is a skill, and it requires your constant efforts in self-education and practice.

I learned to NEVER FORGET THE FUNDAMENTALS. Yes,

I rudely put that in caps, because it's easy to forget. As you learn more and more fancy things about the art and craft of writing, you might be tempted to think that you're so damned talented that you don't need such tired rules as "keep it brief," and "write every day," and "you can't write if you don't read." You should absolutely explore the outer edges of your abilities, and experiment with other ways to do things. But the fundamentals are your home, and you should always return to them.

I learned that you have to enjoy yourself when you're writing. Because if you didn't enjoy writing it, I can guarantee you not many people are going to enjoy reading it. If you're not enjoying yourself, then something is wrong. Maybe you do better when you write hungry. Or write at midnight. Or write at the butt-crack of dawn. Maybe drinking too much the night before turns off your creativity. Then again, maybe it turns it on. Whatever it is, find what's stolen your joy, and get it back. Which leads nicely into my last big lesson learned...

I learned that you need to get good at diagnosing and trouble-shooting yourself. You are going to have days, even weeks—hell, sometimes even months—where the words just aren't flowing. Don't spend this time fretting about the whims of your "muse." And don't worry that you've "lost your touch." You haven't. Professional basketball players don't just forget how to play basketball, and writers don't just forget how to write. Instead of worrying and getting frustrated, take some time to inspect your process and your story structure. It might be a plot point two chapters back that just doesn't make sense, and is taking the story down a road that you subconsciously know is all wrong. It might be a character whose motivations are inconsistent, and leave them feeling deceptive, or shallow. Or it may have something to do with you, your schedule, or your process. Treat yourself like a machine that needs a tune-up. Know your craft, like that old man down the street knows his 1965 Mustang, so that you can get under the hood and intelligently know how to get things running again.

D.J. Molles, *New York Times* and *USA Today* bestselling author of over twenty novels, including The Remaining series, as well as the Lee Harden series, and the Godbreaker Trilogy.

DJMolles.com

LYNN MORRISON

LIKE MANY WRITERS, I started writing for myself. I was a stay-at-home mom with a newborn, living in a foreign country. Writing offered me the chance to continue to use my voice. I'd read back over my words and be astounded at the sheer brilliance that flowed from my fingertips.

And then, one day, after months of writing, I got brave enough to submit my words to an editor. When I opened the returned document and caught sight of the tracked changes, tears welled in my eyes almost to the point of blindness.

To my horrified surprise, I was not nearly as witty and snarky as I thought I was. My long descriptive phrases were unwieldy for the reader. Many of my jokes didn't land at all. Those logical leaps turned out to be black holes for anyone who wasn't living in my head.

Little did I know, but that was a defining moment in my writing career. I stood facing two doorways. I could choose to ignore her advice and continue on, blithely ignoring the faults she'd illuminated. Or, I could embrace her feedback and find out how to make my stories resonate with people other than me.

In order to succeed, I grew a thick skin. That is the only reason I am here today, still writing, more than a decade later.

When you choose to write for others, you must open your heart and mind to their response. Can they picture the world you describe? Do your characters grow from a string of words and quotes into rounded individuals that people love (or love to hate)? Only a reader can tell you if they do. Only a talented editor can advise you on how to bridge the gap. We are terrible judges of our own work.

That said, you must take great care in finding an editor. This is a lesson I learned the hard way. If I could go back in time, I'd etch these words of advice into a mirror and hang it over my desk.

A great editor wants you to succeed

The above phrase seems obvious at first glance, but trust me when I say there is a lot sitting underneath. I am not fully convinced that all editors want their writers to achieve success. Many see their role as one of a gatekeeper. They tear down the writer until there is so little left of the writing dream that they have no choice but to quit. Those editors should be razed from the earth. A great editor wants you and your work to soar. They must be willing to provide as much advice and guidance as they can to make your work better.

This isn't to say that a great editor will simply rubber stamp all your ideas or attempts at writing. There have been many times when I've stretched beyond my current capabilities. A bad editor would tell me to give up. My fantastic editor sent me back to the classroom. "Read these books to see how authors accomplished what you want to do. Study these craft books to better understand how to approach your project."

A great editor helps you realize your vision

In my naivety, I assumed that editors were there to help you fix your grammar and punctuation. It wasn't until I worked myself into a plot knot that I discovered they can do so much more. Editors understand story engines. If your tale fails to move the reader from start to finish, a great editor will know why.

However, it isn't their craft knowledge that makes the big difference. It is their ability to look at your story with a sense of dispassion. They aren't bothered by throwing out hours of plotting and writing if it means getting a better story at the end.

One of the kindest gifts my editor gave me was asking what my big story idea was. "Move it up to the 30,000 foot level. What is the core idea you want to convey?" With my answer in hand, she helped me to hack away the gnarls of detail, whittle away the rough edges, and smooth the end result until I had a story that was worthy of display. More importantly, it was a story I could see from beginning to end.

You are never too good to get by without an editor

After ten books or so, I noticed my editor's comments growing more and more sparse. My confidence grew in the opposite direction. I was one hundred percent sure that I was nailing this writing thing. I didn't need to run my outlines past my editor, or even those early chapters. I could write the entire story and present it to her, complete and ready for her blessing.

She ripped a giant hole in chapter one and sent the draft back without going any further. What was my mistake? I had, once again, forgotten about the reader. I wrote a story I loved and everyone else who read hated. It is the only time in my life I've thrown away an entire draft and started again from scratch.

It turns out that those early conversations with my editor ensured the reader stayed at the forefront of my mind. When I cut her out of the process, I erased their voice as well.

Finding a great editor is no easy task, but it is a necessary one. When you forge a partnership with an editor, you must treasure that relationship as though it were a core friendship. Look for the spark of chemistry, relevant knowledge, and a firm hand. Then hold tight to that connection for as long as you can.

Lynn Morrison lives in Oxford, England along with her husband, two daughters and two cats. When she's not writing cozy mysteries and urban fantasy, she's likely curled up with the cats reading.

LynnMorrisonWriter.com

DAVID RICCIARDI

BLOND HAIR AND BLUE eyes. Sweet and sour. Summer and winter. Whether you're scouting a mate, savoring a meal, or feeling the change of seasons, contrast makes life more interesting—and it makes writing a hell of a lot more interesting.

Whether it's sentence structure (long sentences followed by short ones). Pace (action followed by downtime), or the writing itself (a combination of narrative, dialogue, and action), varying what you put in front of a reader will keep her interest and keep her turning pages.

Have you ever heard a song repeat nothing but the same notes and lyrics over and over? Probably not—and for a good reason. Even "Happy Birthday" has some contrast. That epic third verse where you insert the name? We wouldn't be singing the song a million times a year without it.

I was fortunate to have Jack Romanos, a publishing industry icon, read a draft of my first novel before it was published. I'd taken great pains to put the hero's life in danger for the entire book, and the plot was *Non-Stop Action!!!* I was psyched.

Jack? Not so much. "It's exhausting," he said.

The former Simon and Schuster CEO explained that not only was it hard for a reader to sit on a razor's edge for a 100,000 word novel, but it also made the character one-dimensional. All the hero did was take action to stay alive—and while survival could still be the overarching theme of the story—it couldn't be all of it. When things slow down, readers have a chance to see a different side of their hero, to learn about his history and his desires, his flaws and his failures. Adding sub-plots and varying the pace of my story made it more interesting—just like driving a twisty mountain road is more interesting than driving a straight, flat, mind-numbingly-dull stretch of highway. The contrast holds your attention.

Not only should the plot have a lot of contrast, the chapters should as well. It's rare that a good chapter is all narrative, all dialogue, or all action. It doesn't have to be equal thirds, but a nice mix of the three allows the author to set the scene, escalate the conflict, and resolve it in a way that keeps the reader's brain fully engaged.

It's the same thing with sentences. Strings of long sentences tend to blend together, while alternating long, descriptive sentences with short, declarative sentences will capture a reader's attention. Trust me.

Hopefully we've established that plot, chapter, and sentence structure are critical areas for contrast, but I spend the most time choosing words that complement each other. When I wrote above about the hero's efforts to "stay alive" and also about "survival", I could have used the word "survive" both times, but I varied the phrasing to make it less repetitive. Otherwise, you can end up with a bland string of blandness. I even mix up dialogue tags—the most intentionally forgettable of all words—by alternating my choices based on the rhythm of the exchange, e.g.

"It's exhausting," said Jack.

"It's exhausting," he said.

"It's exhausting," Jack said.

Jack said, "It's exhausting."

I won't lie. I have a lot of OCD tendencies—but I've learned to embrace them. Case in point: When I'm creating an outline, I literally plot the arc of my stories on a timeline. It usually looks like a mountain range. There are peaks and valleys, occasional plateaus, and plenty of crevasses. Like everything in life, of course there are exceptions. It often makes perfect sense to have two action chapters in a row or repeat a phrase for emphasis, but embracing contrast will help you reach writer's nirvana—where your reader simply must turn the page to find out what happens next.

A keen outdoorsman, David Ricciardi incorporated many personal experiences into Warning Light. He's backpacked through the mountains of the western United States and Alaska, received extensive training from law-enforcement and US special operations personnel, and once woke up for a 2 AM watch aboard a sailboat only to discover that it was headed the wrong way through the Atlantic sea lanes in heavy weather, with one of the crew suffering from hypothermia. In addition to being an avid sailor, David is also a certified scuba rescue diver and a former ski instructor. Warning Light is his first novel.

Facebook.com/RicciardiBooks

WHO SAYS IT'S TOO LATE?

"You are never too old to set another goal or to dream a new dream."

— C.S. Lewis

ERIC THOMSON

I BECAME A PUBLISHED author — or perhaps it would be more accurate to say I stumbled into it — later in life than many and was in my early fifties when my first book came out. At that time, I'd already completed a successful military career and worked as an information technology executive responsible for a large organization and budget.

Nothing in my background hinted at me becoming an author. For instance, I have a business degree and was a chartered professional accountant, hardly the sort of education that might seem conducive to something like writing science fiction. Yet in my late twenties, well before ebooks and the rise of independent publishers, I'd entertained hopes of quitting the career path I was on and becoming a full-time writer.

To my sorrow, I gave up on that after shopping the best two of my five manuscripts around without success. But over the following two decades, I pulled those manuscripts out every few years and polished them lovingly. Yet I couldn't find the courage to hunt for an agent or a publisher. It simply seemed too daunting when I was already busy with increasingly heavy professional responsibilities.

Then, quite by accident in late 2014, while chatting about this and that, a colleague and friend mentioned Kindle Direct Publishing. I'd never heard of it, nor had I ever read an ebook, let alone owned a reader. But it piqued my curiosity enough that I figured I'd have nothing to lose by publishing the two stories I'd revised over and over.

That I was totally ignorant about the publishing industry or the rules of writing fiction, let alone creating a suitable book cover, didn't deter me. I think my ignorance actually helped, because I didn't spend much time second-guessing myself and getting cold feet.

To my astonishment, those novels took off — modestly but enough to give me heart — and became the first installments in two long-lived series that found a following.

By the time I wrote and published the second installments for each, working evenings and weekends, I realized I had something I could parlay into a new career, the one I'd been dreaming of in my late twenties.

A year and a half after publishing my first two novels, I sat down with my wife, and we studied our financial situation, considering the rapidly growing income from my books. The stress of my corporate career was taking a heavy toll on my health, and I needed a way out. We quickly realized that if I kept writing at the same rate and my small, but growing readership kept buying, I could afford to retire and devote my life to my novels while building a successful publishing business.

A little over three years and several novels later, I reached the point where the accountant in me decided it was time to incorporate the business for tax reasons. The speed with which I'd reached that point was nothing short of breathtaking.

And so, in my late fifties, I found myself not just a successful military science fiction writer who'd learned the ins and outs of the business, but also the president and general manager of a publishing house. That my wife came along for the ride was an added blessing. She's our company's vice president and editor-in-chief, and since retiring from her full-time job, she also heads our newly established audiobook division.

Am I living the dream I had as a young man? More than I could ever have expected, even if it's later in life. I don't know what would have happened if I hadn't taken a chance back in 2014 to forge my career as an author, with all the attendant pitfalls. However, I'm sure it wouldn't have been as satisfying a life as I'm living now.

Don't ever think it's too late to try. If you have a story in you, get it out, polish it with love, find people you trust to help, and once that first book is ready, put it in front of readers. By doing so, you might make an old dream come true.

But only if you take that first scary step into the unknown. I didn't expect to become a successful author and publisher, yet here I am, with over two dozen published novels in five different series. And all because I took a chance and tried.

Eric Thomson is the pen name of a retired Canadian soldier with thirty-one years of service, both in the Regular Army and the Army Reserve. He spent his Regular Army career in the Infantry and his Reserve service in the Armoured Corps.

ThomsonFiction.ca

B.J. DANIELS

HERE'S WHAT I'VE LEARNED. Writers write. Some write hoping to be rich and famous. I write because I can't NOT write. My husband will tell you that I write all the time. After 30 years of being on deadline, he actually thinks I'll retire at some point.

125 books and more than 40 short stories later, I intend to write as long as I'm able or until I no longer have stories to tell. I believe writers are born this way. They have a love for a blank sheet of paper or an empty computer screen. They have stories percolating in their thoughts all the time. They can't not write.

For so long I thought everyone had stories going on in their heads. I was shocked when I found out otherwise. I asked them, "What do you think about?" They all had to think about that. ☺

I didn't start out wanting fame and fortune either. I never dreamed I'd have such an amazing writing career. I just wanted to tell stories after growing up in a family of storytellers (read: born liars and dreamers). For me, it has always been suspense, probably from growing up watching old mystery movies and westerns with my father. Now I write what I love, Montana, where I live, and mysteries and romance.

Nor is it ever too late if a person is determined to write. I was 47 when I sold my first book. It was also the first book I ever wrote.

For 20 years though, I'd been working at a newspaper writing. I'd learned to write tight, on deadline and to just put in what the reader needed to know. That was the best training ever.

I started with short stories, selling to Woman's World. The editors there kept saying: Tone down the adventure. Still I sold almost 40 before a friend told me about a new line called Harlequin Intrigue, that had both adventure and romance.

I wasn't sure I could do the romance. I just wanted the adventure. But I soon learned that having a hero and heroine in the conflict added to the story. I also learned that there is varying degrees of romance.

A writer just has to find his or her niche – and not follow the crowd. I don't write like my friends even though we are all in the same genre, writing for the same publisher. I believe in writing my stories – not trying to tell someone else's.

Nor is there only one way to write. I remember a writing class I took that required us to fill out a character sheet telling everything we knew about our hero before we'd written a word. I just sat there. I didn't know anything about my hero because I hadn't met him. I hadn't written him yet. I'm not a plotter.

My editor would love it if I were a plotter. But the only way I can write a story is to sit down and start writing. Once my characters stand up and start talking, they'll tell me what's going on. They know better than I do. I'm a seat-of-the-pants writer or a pantser as they call it. I've tried to plot before I write, but it doesn't work for me. I like being surprised by my characters. I get goose bumps when I realize who the killer is – deep in my story.

I think the main thing I've learned is not to let anyone tell you there is only one way to write stories, only one way to get published, only a certain genre to write for.

The best advice I can give is to find your own way. Write what's in your heart. Write what makes you happy. Write because you love writing. All of that will come through in your story. If you love what you write, someone else will.

And don't give up. Always keep learning. Always keep reading. Always tell the most honest story in you. The story that no one else could tell because no one else has lived your life.

New York Times and USA Today bestselling author B.J. Daniels

BJDaniels.com

BILL THOMPSON

AS A CORPORATE ENTREPRENEUR buying, selling and running companies over four decades, I told friends that I'd never retire. Sixty-five was just a number, and I was comfortable working, traveling with my wife of forty-two years and enjoying a great life with friends, food, wine and cigars. Life was good and the future was bright. Until one day—one hour—in a doctor's office in Houston, Texas.

After a year dealing with various issues in her hands and legs, my wife was diagnosed with a rare neurological disease for which there is no cure. "How much time?" we asked, and we learned the earth-shattering truth. She'd be gone in twelve months.

As the weeks passed, I transitioned from executive to caregiver, spending more and more time at home with her, and finding time to finish a novel I'd begun thirty years earlier. She died not long after its publication, and after everything that had happened in the past twelve months, I decided not to return to the "real" world. We sold the company and I started writing book number two, having no idea if this would be a hobby to pass the time or a career. All I knew was that I enjoyed writing novels.

The books came slowly at first—one a year, then two, then three— and they spanned two genres. My early books are archaeological thrillers in the style of Indiana Jones, while my later ones are light horror—ghost stories with a supernatural touch, mostly set in Louisiana's Cajun country. Today I have twenty-two books in print and ebook that have won a total of twenty-three awards. My second career as a novelist is flourishing, and the rewards are truly worth the effort.

I'm an "indie"—an independent or self-published author. That means you won't find my books in airport stores, but I have more control over content, covers and royalty income. Traditionally published authors give up flexibility, and even if a major publishing house accepts your book for publication, the marketing and promotion are still your responsibility. If you're a James Patterson or Clive Cussler, the rules change. Your publisher will put millions on the line to promote your latest release, but the reality of life is that most writers will not achieve international best-seller status. In fact, most won't even make enough to pay expenses.

My books are published through a subsidiary of Amazon called KDP. They are available on Amazon and my website as paperbacks or ebooks, and because I have developed a significant following of loyal fans, I'm making a good living doing something I enjoy.

When I transitioned to writing, the motive wasn't pecuniary. I loved telling a story and I wanted something to fill the time I used to spend at the office. In short, I needed a sense of purpose. As I wrote book after book and the years went by, I found everything I wanted—income bolstered by an ever-growing backlist of titles, a structure in my life thanks to goal-setting, managing my daily writing time and ensuring there was plenty of room for my new wife and me to have lunches, travel and enjoy life…and for me to have a cigar with friends and a martini every afternoon at five.

Writing is fulfilling in a different way than corporate life was. I get an instant performance evaluation every time a reader posts a review on Amazon. I've received thousands of them, and I'm grateful that most of mine are five stars and positive. The negative ones I read and let go. I can take criticism, and you can't please everybody. Some negative reviews help by pointing out an inconsistency or grammatical error. Once a reader gave me a one-star review because he didn't realize the word "novel" meant the book wasn't true. See what I mean? You can't win 'em all.

I've seen estimates that more than a million new books are posted on Amazon a year. Most are self-published like mine, and Amazon founder Jeff Bezos said less than a thousand of those authors will ever make a six-figure income. That's fine with many authors. Some write because they've always wanted to create a book. They pass them out to friends and family and can be justifiably proud of their accomplishment. Some business executives write non-fiction books to distribute to their customers.

My writing goals changed dramatically over time. Initially, I spent a few hours each day putting words on paper. I set challenging goals and pushed myself to finish books more quickly and efficiently, and I enjoyed the satisfaction of writing those last closing words and sending the book off for editing and eventual publication. But once readers began posting positive reviews and I realized people really liked what I was turning out, my writing transitioned from a hobby to a career. Now there were new goals, based on what genre sold best (ghost stories for me) and how many quality stories I could turn out a year (two or three, it turned out). I set new deadlines that allowed me to give my readers more of what they—and I—wanted.

The decision to manage your life as a business, especially in the so-called "retirement years," comes with unique challenges. I was surprised to find that one of mine was dealing with self-imposed deadlines. As a corporate executive, I worked within the framework of deadlines all the time, but this was different. As an independent author, everything about the process is on me. I decide when my book will be released, what advance marketing and publicity I'll do, and how early I send pre-release notices to the thousands of readers who've signed up to receive emails and blogs.

Once I set the release date, everything else must happen on time. Most of my income is derived from book sales on Amazon, and missing a scheduled release date on their website carries serious consequences. Failure to release on time disappoints readers and is unprofessional, and that's the most important part of all. To be taken seriously, an indie author must be equally as professional as traditionally-published novelists.

Self-published authors face relatively low barriers to entry, but not everyone is destined to write a novel. I've found you need a fertile imagination, a knack for spinning a tall tale, and an excellent command of English (or whatever language you'll be writing in). If English class in high school wasn't your bag, and basic writing skills aren't in your toolkit, it's unlikely you'll enjoy—or become successful at—being a novelist.

There are tools in every trade. Mine include a MacBook Air laptop, a big monitor and a software program called Scrivener, which is a godsend to authors. Many novelists do it the old-fashioned way, using longhand, dictation or a typewriter, but I'm afraid my patience and type-A personality aren't suited for that. Give me a computer and a writing program that simplifies my life and I'm happy.

I have outside resources too—a terrific cover designer, a proof-reader and editor, and a few "beta readers" who read my proof before publication and provide feedback. They are critical to the process, but you must be sure you choose people who can be honest and objective. Don't use your mother or your fishing buddy or your friend from the sports bar. Find people who enjoy reading your genre and will give you frank, unbiased criticism. Some authors join beta teams, pairing with another author to exchange honest critiques of style and content.

I love what I've done in the ten years since I turned sixty-five. Sometimes I ask myself when this will end. Will it be when life deals me the cards that let me know it's over? My wife and I learned a lot from the pandemic. I wrote five books during the two years I was cooped up in my office, but now we want to be out traveling and enjoying life with friends and family. I won't publish three books in twelve months again. I'm slowing down, but I doubt I'll ever quit unless circumstances force me to.

At seventy-five, turning out novels keeps my mind active and gives me purpose. When I need a boost, reading reviews from my followers does the trick. And my wife and biggest booster is always making sales. Everywhere we go, she ensures people know I'm an author and that my books are available on Amazon and my website.

These days life is fulfilling and filled with promise. I have more story ideas than I can ever write, and I'll keep doing this until something changes in my life. I just hope it's not anytime soon; I'm having way too much fun!

Bill has always had a burning interest in archaeological finds, mysteries of the past, unexplained things in the jungle and stories of adventure in remote places. Over the years he traveled extensively around the world and visited sites such as Machu Picchu, Stonehenge, Avebury, Egypt, Petra and many ancient Olmec, Aztec and Maya cities in Mexico, Belize and Guatemala, which comes through in vivid detail with his writing.

BillThompsonBooks.com

IT'S A JOB, OR IS IT?

"The only way to do great work is to love what you do. If you haven't found it yet, keep looking. Don't settle."

— Steve Jobs

MARY MONROE

PURSUING A DREAM IS free. You can fantasize about anything you desire, no matter how farfetched it seems. But despite how hard you work to fulfill your dream, there will be obstacles along the way. However, they can provide a lot of motivation. I know now that if I had not encountered any obstacles, I would not have worked so hard to become a published author.

I lived the first few years of my life in rural Alabama in a shabby old house with four generations of relatives. My folks were semi-illiterate and worked menial jobs. They believed we were blessed because we had our health, enough to eat, lots of friends, our church, and a roof over our heads. With so many "blessings", I didn't know why I wanted more out of life. I wanted to share my opinions and ideas with the world. Adults scolded me for asking questions about other lifestyles and cultures. They insisted that those things were of no use to people like us.

I had always had a vivid imagination, but I wanted to develop it even more. We didn't have a television and the nearest library and movie theater were in the next town. I couldn't patronize either one anyway because I was black and both were for whites only. Without the enhancement of library books and movies, I gleaned what I could from radio programs. Other ideas came to me out of nowhere.

One of my favorite pastimes was visiting the local dump where poor kids went to root through the trash. My playmates and I collected discarded toys, and I occasionally stumbled across books with pages still intact. After I had read them, they went back in the trash. My folks believed that everything we needed to know was in the Bible, so it was the only acceptable book in our house. The only other "reading" material I had was our mail order catalogue. I'd read the product descriptions and gaze at pictures of the models and make up stories about their lives.

Before I started elementary school, I knew I wanted to write for a living. Everyone scoffed and compared writing to hobbies like fishing and collecting recipes. They advised me to pray for a future that would include the basics: a real job, a husband, and babies. I wanted those things eventually, but becoming a published author was a dream I was determined to fulfill. I didn't receive any encouragement and was told, "There ain't no little black girls getting paid to write stories." My response was, "This little black girl will."

My prediction came true when my family moved to Ohio many years later. We had a television and I was finally able to get a library card, so I had access to creative nourishment. I worked hard and sold my first story to a confession magazine at the age of fifteen. Each time I sold a new one, people praised me and asked for loans. But they never read any of my published stories. I didn't care because I was so happy to see my words in print.

I enjoyed writing stories with attention-grabbing titles like, "My Husband and His Mistress Tried to Kill Me with Voodoo" "I Married My Rapist" and "I Was the Lonely Hearts Club Swindler." My grandfather reminded me that I was a Christian and should write a story with a religious theme. That night I wrote, "A Homosexual

Preacher Stole My Husband." The magazine editors forwarded fan mail to me from their readers. That gave me such a big head, I decided to start writing novels.

A month after my high school graduation, I went to work at a factory. That same week, I sent my first full-length manuscript to four publishers and four literary agents. Each one sent me a form rejection letter. I didn't receive any sympathy from my friends and co-workers. They teased me so much, I became a closet writer. I only wrote on my lunch hour at work and when I was alone.

I didn't know *why* nobody wanted to publish my book so I made the same mistakes over and over. What I didn't know was that I was doing everything a writer shouldn't do. I submitted query letters and manuscripts with misspelled words, bad grammar, and missing pages. One agent was so familiar with my name that when I stopped pestering him, he sent me a rejection letter addressed to another author!

I collected an average of ten rejections a week for years. Most of them were form letters, but every now and then someone took the time to write something personal. A well-known agent sent me a two-page letter that was so brutal it shook me to the core. Not only did he point out everything he didn't like about my manuscript, he advised me to forget about writing. I stayed up that night and revised the same material. I sent it to four more agents. Three didn't even respond. The fourth one stuck a yellow post-it on the first page of my query letter and printed two words in capital letters: NO THANKS. Some of my rejections are almost as old as I am (I received the first one when I was twelve-years-old). The last time I counted, the total was over two thousand. I probably could have cut that number in half, if I had known what I know now decades ago.

I eventually moved to the San Francisco Bay Area where some of my favorite authors resided. I sent letters to them and begged for information that would help me publish my first novel. Danielle Steel, Alice Walker, and Anne Rice advised me to pick up reference books on writing from libraries and bookstores. I was amazed to discover information about everything from how to write a query letter to tips on grammar.

Once I started following the rules, things changed dramatically. The naysayers who had been teasing me for years were as dumbfounded as I was in 1985 when I published my first novel, *The Upper Room*. They thought I had given up "that writing foolishness." But most of them demanded autographed free copies. One person's only comment was about the cute book cover. Another one eagerly pointed out a misspelled word. To this day, only a handful have read the whole book. I was not able to land a contract for my second book right away, so the teasing resumed and I became a closet writer again. I had no idea it would take *fifteen* years to publish my second novel.

I submitted several new projects to Toni Morrison. She was my idol and an editor at Random House at the time. She didn't accept any of my work, but she gave me some great editorial assistance. She also told me to look at rejections as nothing more than detours.

The tide finally turned in 1999. My new publisher promptly accepted *God Don't Like Ugly* and published it in October 2000. A few weeks later, they offered me another contract to write two more books. The rest is history. I have more than two dozen bestsellers under my belt now, and more in the works. I have also received some very prestigious recognition, including the Maya Angelou Lifetime Achievement award.

My sixth novel, *God Don't Play*, landed on the *New York Times* bestseller list in 2006. When I went to New York to attend a reception and sign books, the same mean agent who had sent me that nasty two-page rejection letter showed up. He congratulated me with a sheepish grin, purchased three copies of my book, and told me he was glad I had not taken his advice and given up writing. I thanked him and told him that his harsh words had motivated me even more.

I write full-time now, but the same naysayers I grew up with are still reminding me that writing is a hobby, not a real job. Despite my success, they tell me on a regular basis about openings at the post office, factories, pizza parlors, and retail stores, and how they would offer more job security for me than my "trying to be a writer."

At a family gathering several years ago, I overheard a conversation between two of my relatives. One bragged excessively about my younger sister landing a management position at a drug store. When my name came up, her response was, "Poor Mary. She ain't found another *real* job yet. She don't do nothing but write books."

Mary Monroe is the award-winning and New York Times bestselling author of over 20 novels, with over one million books in print. She is a three-time AALBC bestseller and winner of the AAMBC Maya Angelou Lifetime Achievement Award, the PEN/Oakland Josephine Miles Award, and the J. California Cooper Memorial Award.

MaryMonroe.org

D.V. BERKOM

TREAT YOUR WRITING LIKE a business. Don't try to do everything yourself. Outsource things that other people can do better: cover design, editing, etc. Your books will look much more professional, which is huge in this super-competitive market. Also, you need to think of your books as a product. That takes the emotion out of it, at least for me. If you're going to run a business that involves your writing, which by itself is an intensely personal act, it's helpful to reduce your sensitivity/reaction to the vagaries of the marketplace.

It's awesome, fulfilling, HARD WORK. Realize going in that you'll need to learn about advertising, production, formatting, presentation, income and expenses, etc. You are a small business—you need to learn how to run that business profitably. And do your research—know what readers expect in your genre, and give it to them in your own way. Also, don't expect everyone to love your work. That's just setting yourself up for disappointment.

Realize, too, how much writing income fluctuates, and figure out how to mitigate big swings. E.g., managing expenses, visibility, production, etc.

Be kind to yourself, but find a way through the difficult times. The first six or so weeks of the COVID lockdown I found it extremely difficult to concentrate on anything but the news and making sure everyone in my household was doing all right. But then I got fed up with myself, planted my ass in the chair and made myself start a new book, and the words started to flow.

That goes for every book. None of them will happen the same way. When I was first starting out I was a pantser (seat-of-your-pants writer) and just winged it. Bad idea, at least for me. I wrote myself into a lot of corners and spent way too much time trying to find my way out. Now, I do a kind of hybrid-style where I start with pen and paper and sketch out a timeline to see if the idea has legs. Then I'll do a loose outline on my laptop, where I hit the highpoints of each chapter followed by some initial research. Then I dive in, writing 5-6 days a week, allowing myself to revise at will. Just having an idea where I'm going helps me stay on track and complete the first draft quicker.

Try different things to build your writing muscles: length, genre, point of view (POV). Learning how to write novellas was like boot camp for writing lean—to strip out all but the most essential information. This has two purposes: one, you don't waste the reader's time with unnecessary fluff; and two, it allows the reader to become more deeply involved in the story by using their imagination to fill in more details. I still apply these same principles for my longer works—my main rule is to NEVER bore the reader. Another one is to never underestimate reader intelligence. I think the recent surge in the popularity of novellas is partly a product of how easy it has become to access content. We're reading on our phones while we're standing in line or waiting at the doctor's office, and shorter works are great for that. I don't think novellas and short stories cannibalize longer novels, though. Data shows there is still a huge market for novel-length works.

More stuff I figured out the hard way:

1. Write a series.

2. After you've written at least 3 books in that series, make the first book free or at least run regular sales.

3. Take advantage of every free promotional opportunity you're comfortable with to get your name out there.

4. Have an easy to navigate website showcasing your books and buy links.

5. Engage with readers and other authors. Comment on blogs and build relationships with bloggers/ reviewers.

6. Start a monthly (or weekly) newsletter, even if it's only going out to Aunt Martha or Cousin Joe. Many of the email providers like Mailerlite or Mailchimp have a free option when you start out. Your subscriber base is one of the most important pieces of your writing empire. These are folks who love your work—treat them well.

7. Join a group specifically in your genre (e.g., Sisters in Crime, RWA, ITW, etc.). Often, you will receive invaluable help from members.

8. Have someone other than your mother/brother/

sister/uncle read your book and give you honest feedback. A great book is the best marketing I know.

9. Write. A lot. Novels, novellas, blog posts, newsletters, whatever you can manage with the time you have. Get to one million words as quickly as you can. One million words is the equivalent to Malcolm Gladwell's 10,000 hours for mastery. Carve out time from your busy day. Make writing important.

10. Read. A lot. In your genre, outside of your genre, non-fiction, etc. It all goes toward making you a better writer.

Bonus tip: HIRE AN EDITOR. I guarantee you will not be able to catch every mistake without one.

DV Berkom is the *USA Today* bestselling author of action-packed, fast-paced thrillers. Known for creating resilient, bad-ass women characters and page-turning plots, her love of the genre stems from a lifelong addiction to reading spy novels, action/adventure books, and crime thrillers.

DVBerkom.com

DELANEY DIAMOND

I WISH I'D TOLD my younger self to prioritize time management. Parkinson's Law states, "work expands to fill the time available for its completion," and it's absolutely true. I learned that the hard way.

One day a few years ago, I looked up at the clock on my computer and was shocked. It was dark outside and almost 9:00 pm. I'd been in my home office since 8:30 that morning—approximately twelve hours! That night I realized my author business had taken over much more of my life than it should, and I needed to make a change.

I took a step back and examined my daily tasks to figure out why I couldn't complete my work in a timely manner. That caused me to recognize two sobering truths: One, I was a terrible procrastinator. Two, I needed to focus first on the task that generated the most income—writing.

In a former life, I was an administrative professional and super organized. Checklists and calendars are my favorite tools, so I went back to the basics and told myself that I work Monday thru Friday and need to leave work at 5:30 pm. I then blocked off hours for specific activities and created recurring appointments on my calendar for work that didn't occur daily.

I worked my schedule and was impressed by the difference. After a couple of weeks, I was less stressed, and I got more work done. Yes, more! I wrote regularly every morning, my to-do list shrank dramatically instead of continuing to grow like it used to, and tasks were crossed out in a timely fashion, which gave me a high from the sense of accomplishment.

I have so much extra time now! On occasion, when I get lost in the minutiae of unimportant tasks or sidetracked by a new class that I want to take or a podcast I just have to listen to, I catch myself and recall how good it feels when I get my writing and other work completed with time to spare. I've learned to be very selective and only do what can fit into my schedule—simply by prioritizing time management and making the best of each work day.

So for new writers, my advice is to prioritize time management. First and foremost, ruthlessly guard your writing time so you can get your writing done on a regular basis—whatever that means for you—daily, on weekends, or at night when the kids are in bed. Get words on the paper because that's how you'll earn your income, and you simply cannot edit a blank page.

Then make a schedule and decide what else you can fit into your day. It's easy to get caught up in all the work we have to do as authors and allow those responsibilities to overrun our lives. But we need balance. Outsource if you have to, but be sure to carve out time for leisure activities, hobbies, and spending time with loved ones.

Believe me, you'll be glad you did.

Delaney Diamond is the *USA Today* bestselling author of over 40 contemporary romance and romantic suspense novels.

DelaneyDiamond.com

KERRIE DROBAN

EVERYONE HAS A STORY, not everyone has a voice. Your *voice* is your power. *What I wish I would have told my younger self...* make writing a habit, do it consistently, don't wait for inspiration, just keep going. Every day is a new opportunity to finish The Book. That's the end game, to *finish*. Without a "product" there is no message, just silence. Set an egg timer, same time, different day. No excuses, no apologies. Don't wait. I had a day job, worked full-time as a criminal defense attorney for over two decades, deconstructing cases, "doing time for the crime" all while incorporating writing into my daily routine. It became a *lifestyle*. Every day for three hours, from 4:00 am to 7:00 am, I sat at my computer in the predawn and composed. This was (and still is) my "witching hour." Compartmentalization is not only a skill it is a necessity. *I would have told my younger self,* writing is not always *fun,* or convenient (sometimes the best ideas need to percolate) but there are moments of pure "magic" when the art of story-telling takes over and maybe for the first time you feel immortal, invincible, alive.

I would have told my younger self to treat writing as a business—to be an "Author." Embrace the value of promotion, speaking, branding and investing. Use every skill you learn—nothing is unimportant or wasted. I studied acting for years and used what I learned about the stage to "get into people's heads," speak well and command an audience. I used what I learned as a lawyer to interpret a set of facts and tell a compelling true story.

I would have told my younger self, writing is not for the squeamish, it takes guts and tenacity and perseverance. Harness the gift. Make it *yours.* And be grateful every day that you get to rearrange words on a page, inspire people, and be the change you want to see in the world.

Kerrie Droban, award-winning author, true-crime television expert, and author of *Vagos, Mongols, and Outlaws*, the basis for the hit TV series *Gangland Under-cover*

KerrieDroban.com

DAN PADAVONA

I WISH I'D UNDERSTOOD how to create a viable commercial product at the start of my career. These days, I view popular genre fiction as a Venn diagram. In one circle, I list the subjects and characters I love to write about. The second circle contains genres with voracious readers. If you crave commercial success, you need to find the overlap between those circles.

For me, this meant cross-referencing dark horror, which I wrote at the beginning of my career, with the more popular thriller and mystery genres. Wonderful opportunities existed in the overlap, from psychological thrillers to gritty serial killer mysteries. Since I grew up reading Thomas Harris and Dean Koontz, writing in these sweet spots came naturally.

That's not to say all writing must be for commercial intent. If you only wish to write for the love of storytelling and share your creations with friends and family, ignore convention and follow your own path, even if it means creating new genres. But the moment you complain about sales or wonder why you haven't attracted new readers, you cross into commercial territory. And that's expected. Writing is difficult. It's common sense that you should receive adequate compensation for your hard work.

I urge new authors to treat writing as a business. As my friend Joanna Penn likes to say, we are creative entrepreneurs. If you aren't comfortable with marketing, become so. Learn how to drive traffic to your books and attract new readers. Between Bookbub, Facebook, and Amazon ads, you can reach new readers in ways publishers only dreamed about two decades ago. In most cases, you receive instant feedback on your efforts. A strong advertisement will produce sales on day one.

As an independent author, I sold over a half-million dollars in books over the last twelve months because I raised my marketing skills until they matched or surpassed my writing acumen. Even if you write for a traditional publishing house, chances are the publisher will expect you to handle much of the marketing. This includes advertising, social media, and building a mailing list. Learn these skills now. Otherwise, you'll find yourself swimming against the tide of authors who know how to sell books.

Dan Padavona is the author of The Wolf of Lake series, The Logan and Scarlett series, The Darkwater Cove series, The Scarlett Bell series, and *Dark Vanishings*, finalist for eFestival of Word's 2016 Indie Novel of the Year award. Several of his Kindle books, paperbacks, and audiobooks rank in the top-20 among Amazon's mystery and thriller categories. He is a proud member of the International Thriller Writers Organization.

DanPadavona.com

MIRANDA SMITH

I WAS IN COLLEGE when I first decided I wanted to write a book. At the time, that was my only goal. Write a book. My first attempt wasn't very good, and it went nowhere, however, that failure taught me valuable lessons that I've carried with me throughout my career.

First, I learned to write the types of books I enjoy reading. I have a slew of mystery and thriller novels on my bookshelf. Most weekends, I'm cozied up watching *Dateline* or true crime documentaries. Once I started writing a crime novel of my own, my dreams of being a published author seemed within reach. The main reason I didn't dive into writing suspense sooner was I didn't believe I was good enough to come up with an amazing, gasp-worthy twist. And I *wasn't* good enough. Yet.

This taught me another valuable lesson: tackle your manuscript one scene at a time. Writing is a process, and while there are many thrilling, artistic, clever moments, there are just as many dull and tedious ones. Inevitably, you will run across a problem in your plot you don't know how to fix, or stumble upon a scenario you're not confident you can write. In my earlier years, one roadblock would be enough to shut down the entire project. My new goal was to finish the manuscript, even if that meant I had to revisit certain scenes over and over again. It often takes many tiresome editing sessions to turn out a polished, entertaining finished product.

And finally, I wish I'd known that a career in publishing entails much more than *writing* a book. That's the fun part, arguably the most important part, but learning what is valuable to publishers and readers is another crucial aspect of the job. Never stop studying the industry. Whether you're researching agents, publishers, or popular trends, it's important to stay informed so that once you've written a spectacular debut, you actually know what to do with it. Study your own genre. Learn what types of stories readers crave and what tropes to avoid. And never stop working on your own craft. Look at each new project as an opportunity to get better.

It takes a lot of hard work. Certainly, more work than my younger self could have imagined. But I'd tell anyone starting out that hard work and big dreams go hand in hand.

Miranda Smith writes domestic and psychological suspense. She is drawn to stories about ordinary people in extraordinary situations, complicated women and dark impulses.

MirandaSmith.com

ERIN FLANAGAN

LIKE MOST PEOPLE I know, I tend to procrastinate chores I don't want to do, be it something as banal as emptying the dishwasher or something as large as working on a novel. I am very much a believer in the carrot not the stick, so when I set out to tackle this problem, I didn't concentrate on the time wasted, but instead looked at just how much time the work actually took.

I operate at a relatively average speed for an able-bodied person, and with timer in hand, I tracked how long it took for me to do those innocuous tasks I kept putting off. The outcome was shocking. That dishwasher I didn't touch for two days as dirty plates and forks piled in the sink and fruit flies invaded my kitchen? It took three minutes to empty. The time it took to fold the clothes in the dryer and start another load? Nine minutes, and yet I'd been known to leave clothes molding in the washer for four days while a second load wrinkled so badly in the dryer, I ended up having to wash both sets again. In both of these cases, it was the procrastinating that made things take so long.

What does this have to do with writing? I'd say everything, because when it got down to it, writing was the thing I procrastinated the most. It wasn't that the task was boring, but quite the opposite; it was too hard, too important, and had too much of my ego wrapped in the job. But I began to wonder, what if I just looked at it as another task?

About six years ago, my accountability buddy and I started timing and tracking our writing, and the information has proven very useful. It's allowed me the opportunity to analyze the data, and to get out of my own way and realize how much writing really is like performing chores. Insurmountable problems in a manuscript such as a plot hole so big it looks like a square mile of scorched earth, can often be cleared up in twenty hours. A last tightening edit can be done in 30. Developmental edits with many issues might go on for 60 hours, but you know what? That's still only a month or two of work at either an hour or two a day.

It took me 497 hours to write my last novel. This is considerably more than three or nine minutes, granted, but also not as many hours as I would have guessed. Now, every day I remind myself: you can write for an hour, or you can waste three hours and then write for an hour, and when I think of it in those terms, it's easier to get to work. Once the dishwasher is empty or the words are written, I feel at peace in a way I hadn't before, and as you can guess, the more time I spend on a task, the bigger the pay off. (Meaning yes, it is way more satisfying to write a novel than empty a dishwasher.)

Does this mean I don't ever procrastinate? Of course not, but I have managed to condense my writing time down considerably. It took me 91 hours to write a draft of my last novel, but that time was spread out of over thirteen months. For the novel I'm working on now, I forced myself to write for an hour or two each day, and I was able to write a draft in just over two months. The number of hours: 88. So it was only three less hours of my butt in the chair, but I saved 11 months by not procrastinating for days and weeks at a time.

So here's what I wish I had learned earlier: writing a book is a lot of work, but it's also just one minute in front of the next. Time is going to pass regardless of whether you're writing, so make your time count. Every day, ask yourself what you want to get done before you lay your head on your pillow. Set a timer and get to work. Write a book and then another and another. Keep track of all you're doing. It will add up, I promise, and faster than you think.

And keep in mind what really matters: the dishwasher, once empty, will fill again, but your words will last forever.

Erin Flanagan's *Blackout* was an Amazon First Reads pick. Her novel *Deer Season* won the 2022 *Edgar Award for Best First Novel by an American Author* and was a finalist for the Macavity Award for Best First Mystery and the Midwest Book Award in Fiction. She contributes regular book reviews to *Publishers Weekly* and other venues.

ErinFlanagan.net

MATT FORBECK

WOW, THERE'S ALL SORTS of stuff I wish I'd known when I started out as a writer. I got taught all the easy stuff in school. You know: how to diagram a sentence, how to show not tell, how to write in a desert-dry academic style that no one likes to read, not even your teachers.

When they realized I was serious about this though — that I really meant to make a living at it — I wish someone had taken me aside and taught me that the actual craft of writing is really just one part of the career.

Being a *working* writer means you're running a small business. That includes doing things like filing taxes, keeping track of your expenses, and even figuring out when the time has come to form a corporation so you can avoid paying extra taxes in the long tradition of all aspiring capitalists.

A writer — really, a freelance creator of any kind — has three jobs. First, you have to *get* the job. That includes things like networking with editors, applying for gigs, answering open calls, or even deciding that you're going to publish the damn stuff yourself. It also means lining up a lawyer, an accountant, and an agent — or negotiating the deals yourself if you have the skills and blind ambition for it.

Then you have to *do* the job. This is the fun part, so you'd better learn to enjoy it. Some writers actually hate writing and only do it for the things they hope it produces, like fortune and glory.

(Please don't do that to yourself. There are far easier ways to pay your rent and get attention. Do the mid-life edition of yourself a favor and try not to get good at doing something you hate.)

Last of all, you have to *get paid* for the job. People who hire writers — especially those who are just starting out and don't know there are even ropes to be shown — often offer lousy deals and sometimes compound that by not bothering to make good on them. Don't let them get away with that, not just for your own sake but for that of anyone else they might try to hire.

If you blow any of those three steps, well, you're out of business, which means you don't get to write anymore. At least not for a living. You can always still do it for fun.

On the other hand, if you can learn to do all three of those things consistently and well, then there's maybe hope for you and your ambitions yet.

Good luck.

Matt Forbeck is an award-winning and *New York Times*-bestselling author and game designer. He has over thirty novels and countless games published to date.

Forbeck.com

THE POWER OF FAITH

"Faith sees the invisible, believes the unbelievable, and receives the impossible."

— Corrie Ten Boom

DAHLIA ROSE

I'VE BEEN WRITING ALL my life, from twelve years old living on the island of Barbados, where I'm from. If you can picture a little girl with either a book or a notebook on her verandah or on the beach with her rowdy older brothers, I was that girl. Watching the water made me dream about what was beyond. There aren't a lot of ways for a girl to become a writer on an island three-hundred and sixty-five miles around. But when my family moved to the United States, I had a family and my career didn't truly start until 2005 with my first contract from a small press. There my journey began, with bumps and lumps along the way.

I remember my first publisher said, there was no black models for cover art so they shaded in a white model…badly I might add. They also went on to steal all my money and then I had to fight to get the rights for my own book to be returned to me. That was only one of my adventures in publishing in the last seventeen years. There's been tons of up and downs, but like waves, swim when you can and tread water when you need to.

Trust me, sometimes you need to have a spine of steel and the mental fortitude to be a writer. For an author of color sometimes the tears seem to fall more often. The battle is hard fought to be successful in a business where we didn't have much of a voice. When I grew up, I was a voracious reader but none of the heroines looked like me, so to readers who were in my position as a young reader, representation is very important. I try to give that now in my books with strong heroines with African American or Caribbean heritage.

Inclusion is the one area in the writing world, that comes hardest to authors like me. Our journeys as any writer, no matter what the ethnicity are a hard fought road, and I commend us all for walking through the gauntlet. But for writers of color, every day is a struggle to find a seat at the table and for 17 years I've fought that battle. I do it willingly and with a smile on my face because this is a career I truly love. Just like everyone in our industry, we want someone to give us a chance. We fight hard, and sometimes those who we put our trust in don't have our best interest at heart. The key is not to give up. The second step is to love your work, and yourself enough to dry those tears, dust yourself off, and start again. If you have that strength within you, why aren't you writing?

In 2003, I had both of my corneas replaced; trust me, don't sign up for that. Before that, I was legally blind and my children were shapes of blurred color. To see them, I had to hold them right up to my face. Since those initial surgeries, I have suffered various rejections of my transplanted corneas, from donor families who gave me such a precious gift. We nicknamed them the little corneas that could because they have not failed me yet.

Last year, I had surgery number six ,and after I healed I was back at work, creating those stories that don't let me sleep. I know you all get what I mean, when characters will not hush for a few hours. If I can literally see my dreams take shape, I know you can too. I've had multiple surgeries on my hands and elbows, carpal tunnel is again not fun, but each time I went back to the words I love.

I don't tell you these things for you to pity me or to shame anyone. It's to tell each of you that even through adversities, I found my path and so can you. What I wish I'd known or have someone tell me when I started my career? That's easy, commit and be present for yourself and your work. No one is going to represent you better than you can. Commit to writing at least five hundred words a day, even if you think it's trash; there are gems in those words. We, who foster this dream to be an artist and to mold heroes and heroines from an idea to write, give yourself the gift of taking some time away from your daily obligations, and put pen to paper. Commit to giving readers the opportunity to see the worlds you create.

While people think that writers are solitary creatures, even if it's online, every writer needs to find their community. The people who will cheer their successes and support us when we fail. Our families may not understand our words, or when we run from a hot shower with an idea we explain in excitement. Then we try to get that precious light bulb that popped into our head on paper without water smudging the words. But your author community will understand, and there are like-minded people who will just be excited as you.

One of the major things I wish I had been told when I was a newbie author trying to swim with the big fishes in the pond, it's okay to be not okay. Every writer's success is not how your life and career needs to be mapped out. Your path is not the same; each journey is different, and it's up to you to find your footing and in a timeline of your choice. I recall looking at others moving forward faster and climbing that ladder quickly compared to me. I wondered what was wrong with my own career choices? I learned that slow and steady wins the race, that I like to craft slowly, then write my words in bursts. Today I consider myself successful because this is my full-time job, well that and going back to college for a Ph.D. in English. What am I thinking, right?

That comes to the very last thing, not something I wish I knew, but instead a nugget of advice I'm passing on to you. Never think you're going to stop learning, that's how your work evolves, that's how you grow as a writer, and your dreams become bigger. To stop learning or to think you know it all, does a disservice to not only your readers, but yourself, because then you stagnate and there are more worlds to explore. Open the doors to your imagination, and give this publishing world hell. Sometimes it's not what we wish we'd known when we started, but what we learn, and pass on along the way.

Dahlia Rose is the *USA Today* best-selling multi-genre author from urban fantasy to romance with a hint of Caribbean spice. She was born and raised on the Caribbean island of Barbados and now currently lives in Charlotte, North Carolina.

DahliaRoseUnscripted.com

CHARLY COX

WHEN I WAS A little girl, I had three dreams: to become the Queen of England, a teacher, and a writer. I've successfully met two of those goals. Spoiler alert: one of them was *not* becoming the Queen. As a grown-up, I've decided to let go of that one, so alas, my focus now remains steadfast on my writing.

Because all kidding aside, writing is hard work, and it takes commitment, discipline, and a strong backbone to trudge through the inevitable rejections from agents, publishers, or readers. No matter how much blood, sweat, and tears you pour into a project, the truth is that not everyone is going to like your work. And that's okay because others will. While part of the writing journey is learning how to get your heart stomped on and then finding a way to stand up and dust yourself off, the other part, the amazing, exhilarating, and scary part, is getting to hand a whole new world over to someone else who gets completely lost in it and comes out the other side feeling all the emotions you'd hoped they'd feel and then some you didn't even know your story would summon.

Writing is learning to face fear, brush off defeat and self-doubt, and giving yourself permission to write really crappy stuff. That's right. You read that correctly. Your first draft is supposed to be a giant mess of "Who the hell would ever read this drivel?" because the next one hundred drafts are what makes your story shine. (Sorry for that little bombshell. There will be periods where you'll rewrite your story so many times, you'll feel like you have more drafts than there are stars in the sky or sands on the beaches.)

Which reminds me—always, always have a pen and paper with you, or if you're the techy type (confession: I am *not*), then something with which you can record ideas as they come to you. In the world of writing, there's little more annoying than solving all your plot issues or coming up with the perfect scene/dialogue/other and not having any way to get that from your head into something where you'll remember it. You'll tell yourself you will. You won't. (Even knowing this, there are times I'll come up with something I think is super exciting or twisty and a game changer and tell my husband about it, and the first thing he asks is, "Did you write it down?" Most of the time the answer is yes. Other times, I insist there's "no way I'll forget it" because it's just an idea. His response is to stop listening to me so he can jot down enough words that will help me jog my memory when I inevitably forget. Because he knows better.)

So, for those of you out there on this writing journey, the best advice I can offer is also the advice I would have liked to have given to my younger self when I first set out on this path.

One: you'll hear tons of advice. Listen to it all and apply what works for your life and your circumstances. (I'm not a fan of the: "You're only a writer *if...*" or "You're not serious about writing *unless...*"). Two: You really need to find a way to shut down or ignore that lying little voice that intrudes inside your head, whispering, "You can't do this. What makes you think you can?" Three: *Really* listen to critiques (which is different than criticism) because if you're talking to the right people, they want you to succeed as much as you do.

That doesn't mean those individuals will always be right. But often they are. So always weigh out their suggestions and comments and see what applies and how it can make you and your writing better. Four: And this is the most important: Keep on keeping on. There will be millions of times for a million different reasons when you'll feel like quitting, but every time you push through, you're one step closer to success. Give yourself permission to take a minute to mourn your setbacks. But then get back up, dust yourself off, and don't give up. Because it'll be one of those times that a door might just be opening for you. And I know because that's exactly what happened to me. One day, I opened my email, fully expecting to see another rejection—only to read that I was receiving an offer for publication. All because I kept on keeping on.

Charly Cox: Bestselling author of the Detective Alyssa Wyatt Crime Thriller series

CharlyCoxAuthor.com

CATHY MCDAVID

SOMEONE ONCE TOLD ME a long time ago there are three kinds of writers: 1) dabblers who play around with writing but aren't serious and don't publish, 2) hobbyists, who publish on a small scale and earn a little income, and 3) professionals, those who consistently produce, actively pursue publication, and get paid for what they do.

At first, the words didn't sink in. Not fully. But eventually I realized I needed to be a professional writer if I had any hope of succeeding in this ever changing, highly competitive, slippery slope publishing industry. When I look back at my nearly twenty-five-year career, there are standout moments when I made a leap forward — leaps that were the direct result of a decision I made or an action I took.

Keep in mind, publishing was an entirely different animal back when I started. The goal of most authors was to sell to a big New York traditional publisher. Self-publishing was looked down on and few people pursued it (hard to believe, I know). But change was on the horizon. E-books were gaining popularity, and, as a result, small presses had started popping up all over the place. Like everyone then, I'd first submit my manuscript to traditional publishers according to my wish list. Avon. St. Martins. Warner. Kensington. And my dream publisher, Harlequin. When they rejected me, and they all did, my next step was to submit to small presses. I fared better with them and eventually had three small press books under my belt. While the experience was great, I wasn't earning much money. In fact, I was losing money by the truckload when you tallied up my expenses. But I loved every minute, and that was what counted. Not to mention, I was gaining a valuable education.

Eventually, I wrote a book I was certain would win me my big break. Alas, it wasn't to be, and the large traditional publishers turned me down. Again. As usual, I sent my manuscript off to a several small presses and promptly received two contract offers within days of each other.

But something stopped me from accepting. After considering the offers at length, I emailed both small presses with my thanks but no thanks. I vowed the next offer I accepted would be from a publisher that paid, at minimum, four-figure advances, produced professional covers, and distributed to bookstores rather than simply selling them online from a website (don't laugh - remember, it was a different time). It took a-year-and-a-half for me to finally sell to a mid-size publisher. I got that four-figure advance and an option for a second book. Granted, the publisher wasn't the biggest fish in the sea. However, doors opened for me. I was finally on my way and all because I chose not to settle.

To be honest, it was hard turning down those small press offers with no better deal in sight. There were days the doubts crept in, and I was convinced I'd made a mistake. During the long wait to sell that book I wrote two more, figuring I'd have something new to submit when I finally got that contract. My strategy paid off, and

I wound up selling four books to two different mid-size publishers, each deal marginally better than the last. But I hadn't reached my goal of being a New York traditional published author. To accomplish that, I had to take another leap.

Around this same time, a lot of my friends were agent hunting. Harlequin didn't require authors to have an agent in order to submit, so I wasn't in the market for one. That said, I wasn't closed to the idea. Having an agent could afford me more opportunities and give me some needed street cred.

What happened next is one of those rare, serendipitous events. I happened to partner on a book with a writer friend — my one and only attempt at co-writing. She was on the hunt for an agent in a big way, and what do you know she landed one! When she called to tell me the good news, she mentioned the agent wanted to represent the book she and I had written together. Well, of course. I was on board. The agent phoned a short time later to discuss the terms of co-representing my friend and I on this one book. The next words that came out of my mouth were a complete surprise to me and, I'm pretty sure, to her, too. I told the agent everything sounded great except for one thing: I wanted her to represent *all* my books, not just the one I'd written with my friend. A full ten seconds of silence followed after which she agreed to look at my work.

To make a long story short, six weeks later I signed with her agency. A year after that, I finally sold to a New York traditional publisher. I sometimes wonder what different course my writing career would have taken had I not mustered my courage and asked the agent for a chance. What's that old saying about luck? It happens when preparation meets opportunity.

I'll never forget walking into a bookstore for the first time and seeing my book on the shelf. Lightning struck. Wait. That's not entirely accurate. I was hooked and wanted to re-experience the feeling over and over. It gave me a clear goal to strive for, and I promptly went to work. FYI, the thrill still hasn't worn off even after fifty-eight plus books. With every new release, I walk into Wal-Mart, take a picture of my book on the shelf, and then buy a copy. Yeah, I admit it. I also move the remaining copies of my book up to eye level.

I have to be honest; my agent and I haven't always seen eye-to-eye. There was this one time in particular when I trusted my gut more than I trusted her advice. Don't get me wrong, she's done right by me plenty. Gotten me higher advances and better terms. But I had this book idea and was convinced it would at last grant me entry into Harlequin's hallowed halls. My agent, not so much. She thought the idea needed a major overhaul. Nonetheless, I pitched the book to a Harlequin executive editor at a local conference, and she asked to see a partial. My agent submitted the partial, but with reservations. She feared another rejection (by now I had a pretty impressive collection of them).

Well, turns out she was wrong. Instead of a rejection I received a request for revisions. And then a request for the full manuscript. Then another revision request. I've lost track of how many. Then, I received one last revision request. That was delivered in person at a national romance writers' conference over coffee with the executive editor and the senior editor for the line. Three months later, I was officially a Harlequin author. I might not have finally realized my long-held dream if I hadn't trusted my gut even in the face of discouragement.

Speaking of meeting with editors at conferences and pitching your book, if I can give only one piece of advice to new authors it would be: network, network, network. Not just with industry professionals but other authors. You never know where a connection will lead you. Nowadays I see a lot of networking happening online rather than in person, especially pitching books during social media events. But the concept is still the same and the results. Get to know the people who can help you. Listen to them. Learn from them. Ask questions. And if you're able, return the favor. Publishing is a small world, and your reputation will follow you everywhere.

Not to sound cliche, but success doesn't just fall into people's laps. It's the result of hard work and seizing the moment. Every milestone I've reached, every dream I've realized, every award I've earned, every accomplishment I can claim and every best-selling status I've achieved, can be traced back to a single moment when I made a decision and took a leap. So, what are you waiting for?

Cathy McDavid, *New York Times*, *USA Today* and Amazon bestselling author, with over 58 titles in print and 1.6 million-plus books sold. Cathy is also a member of the prestigious Romance Writers of America's Honor Roll.

CathyMcDavid.com

CARLY PHILLIPS

I'VE BEEN PUBLISHED SINCE 1998 but actually writing and trying to publish since 1993. In 2002, my book, The Bachelor, was the first romance chosen for a nationally televised bookclub: Reading with Ripa on LIVE! With Regis and Kelly (in the days before Facebook and social media). How? I saw Kelly joking about having a smutty bookclub on her show and sent her a basket with my book. (Note - It's not smut, it's Romance but you get the picture!). My career soared and I rode the ups and downs of NY publishing with various houses until 2013 when I left NY Publishing and made the jump to Indie publishing. I was petrified. I didn't have Amazon access to do preorders. The day my first release came out, I cried and almost begged NY to take me back. Looking back, despite my fear, I'm so glad I made the leap. I trusted my instincts. Trust yours. I set up a team of people - not people who worked exclusively for me but I chose people who specialized (publicist, editing, formatting, uploading, graphics, etc.) and had them all lined up prior to even diving in and writing the first book in my new series. I thought of it as my own little empire. I talked to every friend I knew who'd already gone indie and learned from them. And I learned I love running my own business and being in control. Don't let fear hold you back. I did that for too long before making that jump. Trust yourself. Learn your craft. Learn the business and let yourself fly.

Carly Phillips, *New York Times*, *Wall Street Journal*, and *USA Today* bestselling author

CarlyPhillips.com

ERNEST DEMPSEY

I DON'T WISH I had known anything different when I started publishing. To do so would invalidate my journey to this point and all of the things I've learned.

It is the difficult times that make us better. And those difficult times are also part of the journey, part of what makes you you, and what made me who I am today.

Those things I could wish I had known might have served me in the short term earlier in my career, but I'm certain had I risen faster I probably would have also crashed and never realized what went wrong.

Through constant struggle, testing, failure, and disappointment we are forged in the crucible of author hood—making us better at everything we do.

At the age of 40, my wife and I were having a baby. I quit my job a few days before our daughter's birth, and decided it was time to write books full time.

One year later I was broke, we sold our house, and moved into my parents' home in my brother's old room downstairs.

For fourteen months we lived there, sleeping on mattresses on the floor, bugs crawling around on the carpet, using a tiny shower and with all my clothes in cardboard boxes.

We had nothing but our cars.

The day I walked into my parents' house with my daughter, I broke down in tears. My mom asked what was wrong.

I told her I was fine, that I just wanted my kid to be happy and to have a fun life.

The truth was, I'd never felt more like a failure in my entire life.

I'd risked it all on a pipe dream, and lost everything.

But I kept at it. My wife supported us, and my writing, and we dug out of the hole. Three months after moving in with my parents, I hit the *USA Today* list. Not because of some marketing genius on my part. Because I kept working, kept pushing forward.

The rest is history.

I have a successful book business now, and I am able to live a life I only dreamed about when I worked as a high school guidance counselor.

Never spend your days wishing you'd known something or thinking "if I had only done this."

Do the next thing. And the next thing. Keep working. Keep grinding.

I have bigger dreams for our future. And I'm going to make them happen.

It will require failures, missteps, and disappointment. The greatest successes always do.

Look how many rockets Elon Musk blew up before he got one to work.

Blow up your rockets and laugh every time you do. Because when one reaches the stars, you will be grateful, and better for all those explosions.

Ernest Dempsy, author of The Relic Runner and Sean Wyatt Adventure series. He's also your friendly neighborhood author.

ErnestDempsey.net

KATE HEWITT

WHAT I WOULD HAVE told my younger self… is that no one can tell the stories in your head but you. You have a unique voice and something to offer the world that no one else can. That's not necessarily enough to be successful, but it's an incredible start. Protect and cherish your voice, trust your creative process, and most of all *write*. Write, if not every day, then almost every day, as consistently as you can.

Write without rereading or editing, so you can delve more deeply into your own emotions and put them on the page. Editing can always be done later. And most of all, write to the end. Finish the story, and then start another, because having a dozen first chapters doesn't actually teach you all that much. Writing to the end helps you to learn structure and pacing, to get the feel of how a story—your story—is meant to work, and best of all, you can submit something if it is finished.

Write but also read—read different genres and authors you wouldn't normally pick up, because in reading other authors' voices you discover your own. Write, read, and persevere. The first story may never be published, and maybe not the second, third, or twenty-third, either. A published author once told me when I had finaled in a contest for unpublished authors that everyone who had finaled in that contest previously had sold… eventually. For some it had taken months, for others years, but none of them had given up. A publishing deal might not happen tomorrow or next year or even in the next decade, but if you keep writing, keep growing as a writer, and keep submitting, it will happen one day.

And then I would have told my younger self that when it *does* happen, it's not the end, but rather the beginning—and there will be just as many, if not more, challenges, struggles and disappointments after being published than before—but it will be worth it, and each obstacle is part of the journey. I would have told my younger self, so full of self-doubt and uncertainty, that I really can trust my creative process, and that the story I'm struggling with will unfold in the proper time and way—but I've still got to write it!

Lastly, I would have told my younger self to hold onto my joy. Poor sales, bad reviews, a difficult agent or editor, the folding of a publishing house, the uncertainty of depending on royalties… it can get you down, but ultimately being a writer—a creator of stories—is the most wonderful thing in the world, a privilege and a blessing, and I am so grateful for the opportunity I've been given to share my imagination with the world.

Kate Hewitt, bestselling author of historical and contemporary fiction. Her novels have been called 'unputdownable' and 'the most emotional book I have ever read' by readers.

Kate-Hewitt.com

MEERA KOTHAND

THE BIG BOOKSTORE, THE TV appearances, the huge publishers...

Those don't define whether you're a writer or not.

You're a writer regardless of whether you self-publish, have a publishing deal, blog or write for magazines.

I personally know writers who self-published and earn six and seven figures from their books and those who managed to get a publishing deal and earned pretty much nothing at all.

Let go of the outcome and concept of what you think a writing career should look like. By holding onto a preconceived idea, you close doors which could pave the way for other opportunities.

It's a fantastic time to be a writer with multiple opportunities and avenues. The only thing stopping you is YOU.

You just have to want it enough and work towards it.

Don't buy into the narrative that you can't make a living from creative work. I've always been a lover of words. Always been in wonder of the written word. Dabbled in writing since kindergarten.

But no one including myself ever expected anything to come of it.

Be aware of the stories and narratives that are holding you back from writing. Resist them even if the world around you holds you to them and plays them on a loop.

You're a writer. You'll always be one.

Say it.

Embrace it.

The more you do, the more it becomes your reality.

It becomes the air you breathe, the water you swim in, the words you speak.

Meera is an author and speaker who specializes in making marketing your online business ridiculously simple. She's got seven books on the Amazon bestsellers' list, including *The One Hour Content Plan*, *Your First 100*, and *The Blog Startup*.

MeeraKothand.com

ELIZABETH BROMKE

WHEN I WAS YOUNGER, I figured that becoming a writer—an author—was a pie-in-the-sky thing. A pipe dream. A fantasy. I let it be that, too. I'd start a book or a short story. I'd get hit with a bout of inspiration, whip out a narrative, and email it out to a handful of agents or publishers and I'd remind myself, *this is just a dream. Remember, you're a teacher. You're a normal person. You're not actually a writer.*

It turns out that I was always probably a writer. I just never believed it. I thought it was something that might happen to me, not something that I would make happen. That I would *live*. In fact, it wasn't about inspiration that led to my decision to just commit. It was desperation. I needed something more. I needed to breathe. I needed to cry and to live and I needed something *more*. So, I gave myself a timeline. Thirty days. Write the book. Publish it. See what happens.

Spoiler: nothing happened.

A handful of family/friends bought the book. It simmered down low on the charts, but do you know what? It didn't matter. I had committed. I had decided that I wasn't just a teacher or a normal person any longer. I was also a writer, and so I wrote the next book. And the next. And I kept publishing. And I kept marketing. And I kept *improving*. And I hit a list or two, and I made money, and I gained readers. All of a sudden (well, not really, this was all about two years in), I was breathing and crying and laughing and living. I had all I ever dreamed of.

And now? Well, now I wonder why I waited so long to take a dream and make it come true, because it turns out, dreams aren't just for sleeping through. They're for living.

Elizabeth Bromke, *USA Today* bestselling women's fiction and romance author.

ElizabethBromke.com

DWIGHT HOLING

FACTS FUEL FICTION. CHARACTERS hook readers. Structure spawns creativity. Deadlines produce publication.

Call them simple slogans or maybe even a mantra, but they reside top of mind every time I saddle up and ride, er, write. I learned them over the many years I spent writing newspaper articles, magazine stories, and books on natural history, conservation, and outdoor adventure travel. When I moved over to crafting literary short stories and crime fiction, they proved right again.

Spare me the joke that journalism is the world's second oldest profession and nowhere near as well-compensated as the first. Plenty of creative juice gets spilled reporting the news, whether or not you subscribe to such journalistic techniques as Tom Wolfe's mau-mauing or Mark Twain's never letting the facts get in the way of a good story. Good reportage has its place in good fiction writing too, no matter the genre, whether it's a thriller, romance, or paranormal. Sure, readers read fiction to meet new people, visit new worlds, and live vicariously, but they also want to learn new things that broaden their knowledge and enhance the way they experience the world.

Chiseled on a tablet somewhere is the adage *Write about what you know.* For me, it was no mystery why I reached back to my environmental reporting days for subject matter when it came to writing crime fiction. Characters, conflicts, and very cool stuff were always to be found in the subjects I once covered, and I've learned not only is the natural world a source and inspiration for a mystery series set in the high lonesome of southeastern Oregon in the late 1960s, but also helps lend authenticity to time, setting, and dialogue. Wildlife, weather, and landscape all play integral roles in the arcs of my stories and development of my characters. They provide action, motivation, and revelation.

To create that takes structure, and there's a double meaning to that. Along with developing a story's arc, you need to lock in time so you can be locked in with your characters. They can't talk, they can't do, they can't love and hate, live and die, if you're not there with them every step of the way. In my case, that's 9 to 5 every day of the week with Saturday and Sunday off for good behavior—but only if I've earned it.

Deadlines? Love 'em or hate 'em, you can't live without 'em. This is especially true if you're an indie. Deadlines go along with structure. They both spark imagination. Try viewing deadlines this way: You're trapped in a room. You gotta get out. MacGyver it.

What isn't carved in that proverbial tablet I mentioned is the answer to *Why do you write in the first place?* That's something all writers have to ask themselves, especially when they're starting out. Are you writing because you *want* to be a writer or because you *have* to write? At the end of the day, all writers are storytellers, no matter if the story they're telling is fact or fiction. If there's a story burning inside you, put it out there. I don't mean put out the flames, I mean fan them. Breathe life into the story. Publish it. Let others read it. And then rinse and repeat. There's always another story in you. I'm sure of it.

Dwight Holing, an award-winning author, is the author of The Nick Drake novels and Jack McCoul Capers mystery series, literary short story collections, and numerous nonfiction books on nature travel and conservation.

DwightHoling.com

ROCHELLE B. WEINSTEIN

WHILE I WAS A voracious reader and journal writer from a very young age—often imagining being the next Judy Blume or Danielle Steele—insecurities and doubts plagued me, and I began a career in the music business before sitting down at the age of thirty to write my first novel.

I had no expectations for *What We Leave Behind*. There was a story in me that needed to be told, and I sat down and wrote it. Once completed, the novel sat under my bed until a carpool mom suggested I share it with her book club. Their enthusiasm for the manuscript motivated me to search for an agent where my query letters sat in hundreds of slush piles with rejections such as: You don't know how to craft a novel, the story doesn't resonate with me, or, I'm just not interested in reading any farther. Nothing is more debilitating to an author than an agent's rejection.

Here's where you reach your career crossroads. What do you do with that rejection? Do you give in to it? Do you let it chart your course? This was 2010, and self-publishing was emerging as a viable option for seeing one's book in print. Sure, there were credibility factors. The voices in my head were telling me I wasn't good enough for this industry, but I understood very early on what I wanted out of my writing, and you must know what you want out of yours.

Determined and focused, I self-published *What We Leave Behind* in 2012. Then I followed it up with *The Mourning After* in 2013. Using my marketing and promotional background, I found a way to break through and get my book out there, and with robust sales, I finally had the leverage I needed to capture an agent's attention.

With a seasoned professional advocating on my behalf, I acquired my first publishing deal in 2016 with *Where We Fall*. After that, *Somebody's Daughter* (2018), *This is Not How It Ends* (2020), and *When We Let Go* (2022) followed. During that time, I learned, by accident, that *What We Leave Behind* had hit the *USA Today* Bestseller list back in 2014. This was 2017, and I had no idea. So, to answer the question, what would I tell my younger, greener self? It would be something like this:

You may not always have accolades, positive reviews, or sales numbers to buoy you through the tough times, but believing in yourself and your dream will get you through. Imagine had I given up. Imagine if I didn't take the other path. Having experienced rejection and frustration, finding the will and perseverance to pick myself up and move forward was hard. And while hitting a coveted bestseller list was admirable, I knew not to give it too much weight or let it define who I am. What defines us writers is the effort. The fortitude. The never giving up. Choosing the different door. Finding the best path for *you*. And more importantly, accomplishing this in the face of criticism and judgment with grace, passion, and a willingness to try again, because, after all, writing is re-writing.

If you want to be a writer, here's the best advice I can offer. Shut out the rest of the world and *keep going*.

Rochelle B. Weinstein is the USA Today and Amazon bestselling author of six women's fiction novels. Rochelle spent her early years, always with a book in hand, raised by the likes of Sidney Sheldon and Judy Blume. A former entertainment industry executive, she splits her time between sunny South Florida and the mountains of North Carolina. When she's not writing, Rochelle can be found hiking, reading, and searching for the world's best nachos. She is currently working on her seventh novel.

Instagram:
Facebook: https://www.facebook.com/rochelle.b.weinstein
Twitter: https://twitter.com/rochwein
Subscribe to her newsletter at www.rochelleweinstein.com.

T. B. MARKINSON

I STILL REMEMBER THE wonderful day when I figured out I wanted to be an author.

In the sixth grade, I had to pen a story about Christmas. I really got in the spirit, sitting on a stool in front of a Christmas tree, scribbling by bubble lights. After turning in my homework, I promptly forgot it because it was nearly Christmas, and I had more important matters to worry about, like gifts.

Before winter break, the teacher handed the assignment back to me with a note at the top that said: *When you grow up, you should be a writer.*

I'd never considered that possibility until that moment. I already loved stories, but I hadn't stopped to consider that people created them instead of them magically appearing in books. As soon as the idea struck me, I was sold on the dream.

For years and years, I dedicated time to writing, but I don't think I truly believed it would come true until many years later. 2010 to be exact. I was sitting at a diner in New Orleans, and I wrote down in my journal, *I want to be a writer.*

I can't explain what happened next. Perhaps it was being in a city that had been brought to life to me in books since childhood, and it was my first time visiting. Or maybe it was the ghosts of many previous authors who had walked the streets of New Orleans before me, but I crossed out my words and replaced the sentence with: *I am a writer.* I underlined the word *am* a few times.

At this point, I hadn't been published, but I'd always been writing, and the desire to see my dream come true continued to burn brightly despite a handful of rejection letters.

That lightbulb moment in the diner helped kick me into gear.

In 2011, I moved from Boston to London with my partner who was transferred for work, and I found myself without a full-time office job.

I dedicated the next few years to finishing a book and studying indie publishing.

In 2013, I published my first novel. Since then, I've released more than 30 books, and I support myself with my writing.

I wish I'd known the power of self-belief from the start, although all the twists and turns my life has taken have enriched my story-telling abilities.

One last thing. For all those who encourage others to chase their dreams, like my teacher, it's the best gift you can give another person. Belief is a powerful emotion, and sometimes you need to know others believe you so you can dig deep to find the faith needed to say, *Yes, I can.*

TB Markinson, award winning and bestselling sapphic fiction author with over 30 titles and founder of IHeartSapphFic.com.

JEFF STRAND

IN MANY WAYS, I'M glad I didn't get to peek into the crystal ball. If my sixteen-year-old self had known that I wouldn't become a full-time writer until I was in my mid-forties, he might have said, "Maybe a career in advertising is the way to go!" What kept me going through the very, very, very slow ascent was the certainty that the next year would be THE year! I never gave up on my dream, but I'm not sure how I would've reacted if I'd been told as a teenager that I had about three decades to wait before I was doing what I loved for a living.

What I wish my younger self had known is that sometimes it's okay to compromise. So when the world's biggest romance publisher said that my romantic comedy essentially had too many jokes in it, sent me some free books to get a better idea of what they were looking for, and invited me to resubmit, I wish I hadn't said "I don't want to write this crap!" Oh, sure, I maintained my creative integrity, but getting paid to write is better than not getting paid to write. It certainly would have put me closer to my overall goal than those many extra years at the corporate desk job.

I'm not saying that I wish my books had become passionless, cynical cash grabs. "Write what you love and the money will follow" worked...eventually. But there's also something to be said for acknowledging that publishing is a business, and with the benefit of 20/20 hindsight, I would've made some different decisions with that in mind. You can improve your chances of success without selling your soul.

On the flip side, it would've been super sweet to be able to tell myself in my thirties that my fifties were going to be freaking *awesome*.

Jeff Strand is the Bram Stoker Award-winning author of 50+ books, including *Blister*, *A Bad Day For Voodoo*, and *Wolf Hunt*. *Cemetery Dance* magazine said, "No author working today comes close to Jeff Strand's perfect mixture of comedy and terror." Several of his books are in development as movies.

JeffStrand.wordpress.com

RITA HERRON

MY MOTHER USED TO have a saying – *Can't never did anything.* Her expression stuck with me through life - if you say you can't do it, you probably won't. Positive thinking is powerful. You must believe in yourself for others to believe in you!

I learned the hard way that I had to apply that mantra to my writing.

When I first began my journey, I was a closet writer and kept my dreams to myself. When I finally got up the nerve to tell family, one member laughed at me. That hurt. But I'm a stubborn Taurus and it made me more determined to prove them wrong.

Like most beginners, I had allusions of selling my first book and it becoming a huge success. Yet I knew nothing of story structure, editing, or the business aspect of writing and publication.

Reality came when I joined a writer's organization and gained the courage to submit my story for a critique. While that was painful, it was the first step in my journey to publication.

I realized that like any new job or career change – I was a teacher at the time – it was not going to happen overnight. After all, it took me four years to earn a teaching degree, then years of hands-on classroom experience to become skilled at what I was doing.

Why was this different?

It wasn't.

First, I started reading voraciously to discover the type of books I enjoyed. My aha moment came when I was reading a Tami Hoag book. I was so blown away by her writing, the romance and suspense, that I knew that was the kind of book I wanted to write.

My next step was to attend conferences and workshops where I leaned to ask questions, listen to other authors and learn more about the business from editors and agents who attended.

I found a critique group and learned to accept constructive feedback. Rejections and criticism are difficult, but those prompted me to work harder. While some authors have a book of their heart and are married to their work, I began keeping an idea file with alternate ideas to pitch or work on. While we always think our idea is great, and it may be, you never know if another writer is producing something similar. In more than one pitch session, I heard an editor say they liked an author's idea, but something similar had just landed on their desk. Then the editor asked if they had anything else. So have at least two or three alternate ideas ready to pitch in a sentence or two!

For me that helped with rejections. I didn't feel as defeated because I had another story line waiting. Instead of writing one book of the heart, I tried to put heart in every book.

Slowly I developed my *Voice*. Your voice is your unique way of storytelling, phrasing, and descriptions and is key to standing out amongst a sea of other writers. For me that came with feedback from editors, both positive and negative comments. At the time, I was writing different genres to try and break in. But one editor and agent pointed out that my suspense voice was stronger and stood out so then I started to focus.

I also observed other writers and what they were doing to achieve success. That doesn't mean copying them or their style. It means developing my own. Then came the business side: the more successful authors usually stuck with one genre and built a readership. That meant writing the same type of book, but different each time.

My critique partner and I have a saying: Give the reader what they want. For example, if you've written a romance and readers liked that book, when they see your name again they expect to see another romance. Instead of being a jack of all trades, focus on one and hone your skills there.

You also must make your reader care about your characters. If they don't care what happens to the characters, they'll stop reading. This is another place to make your work stand out. Your main characters/ protagonist needs to be believable and likeable, someone the reader can root for as they face obstacles and challenges in the story.

I still remember the first writing course I took – the teacher wrote the word CONFLICT on the whiteboard and made us repeat over and over: Conflict is Story. Your story should start with conflict. Throw your protagonist into a difficult situation, a major change in their lives, a place where they face problems. The journey for them and the readers is how to overcome that problem, how they face the challenge, and how that challenge changes them. That character growth leads to a satisfied reader!

Some advice I'd offer: Surround yourself with other writers. Only they can understand your process and the ups and downs of the business. Writing can be a lonely job and you need to have the support of others in your field. So network, network, network.

Also grow a thick skin. You will get rejected at some point, probably multiple times. If one person doesn't like your work or has a problem with a certain part, that's one person. But if multiple people give you the same feedback, there might be a problem that you need to address within your manuscript. When people offer suggestions, remember that you don't have to redo it the way they suggested. But you can figure out a way to make changes your own way.

Most of all, never give up. Don't let anyone crush your dreams. I have a wall plaque in my office that says: DREAM IT. WISH IT. DO IT!

And whenever I feel defeated, I hear my mama's voice in my head saying: Can't Never Did Anything!

Rita Herron, *USA Today* bestselling and award-winning author. With over 90 books to her credit, she's penned romantic suspense, romantic comedy, and YA stories, but she especially loves writing dark romantic suspense tales set in southern small towns.

RitaHerron.com

BARBARA NICKLESS

MY KIDS WOULD TELL you I never miss an opportunity to pass along advice. So, I'd—lovingly—try to impart several lessons to my younger self.

First, I would tell my younger self to stay true to the stories of the heart. Don't follow trends or sacrifice what you love in an all-out pursuit of publication. Writing is sometimes (often?) difficult to the point of feeling impossible. If you're listening to that inner voice, following your calling, then you are doing the critical work that will feed your writerly soul along the journey—however long that journey takes and however long it lasts.

Second, oh, younger self, be patient. With the process. With yourself. With the publishing world. This is a long game, but if you're writing the stories you love, having fun, and if you're also continually pushing yourself to improve, then when things break your way, they just might break in a big way. And if not, at least you will have enjoyed the journey. No one can take that from you.

Third, separate your work from yourself. Both have value. But the worth of one doesn't depend on the worth of the other. And neither depends on what anyone else says.

Fourth, strap in for a rollercoaster ride. The only certain thing in a writer's journey is that things will change. Sometimes in ways you'd rather they didn't. Publishers go out of business. Contracts get cancelled. But sometimes they change in ways that are pure magic. A call from an editor. Or a film agent. Do your best to find a middle ground within yourself so that you don't get whiplash during the ups and downs.

Finally, in the wise words of Christopher Volger, the author of *The Writer's Journey,* trust the path. Believe that there are stories you are meant to write. Do the work and have faith that things will unfold in ways you can't yet imagine.

Author of the award-winning Sydney Parnell series. Now out: A new series starring Professor Evan Wilding in *At First Light*. "Barbara Nickless is a superb writer." —No. 1 International Bestselling Author Steve Berry

www.BarbaraNickless.com

WRITE WHAT YOU LOVE OR WRITE FOR THE MARKET?

"A writer who is a pro can take on almost any assignment, but if he or she doesn't much care about the subject, I try to dissuade the writer, as in that case the book can be just plain hard labor."

— Sterling Lord

JACQUELIN THOMAS

I'VE ALWAYS KNOWN THAT I wanted to be a writer. I was terribly shy growing up so writing became my voice. I could put on paper what I couldn't verbalize. Although becoming an author was my goal—I didn't set out to make it a reality until many years later. I wanted to write about people like me, people of color. It wasn't until I discovered Terry McMillian and Beverly Jenkins that the opportunity presented itself.

My path to publishing was fairly painless. Before I submitted my manuscript anywhere, there were several people who advised me to revise my story. They felt it was too dark for the romance genre because the heroine was a survivor of sexual assault. However, while I appreciated the feedback, this was the story of my heart.

I didn't change it.

I secured an agent who was enthusiastic about the project. I received five rejections from publishers before I got the call from Monica Harris, who was with Kensington Publishing at the time. Now twenty-five years later, I would tell my younger self to always trust my gut instincts when it comes to writing. To always write from the heart and not necessarily for the market. There are times when you must defend your stories, even if it means walking away empty-handed.

There have been a couple of times when I felt I sacrificed the heart of my stories to editorial changes I didn't agree with. My readers were not happy and didn't hesitate to tell me. It only took those two incidents to convince me that no one can tell my stories the way that I do. Don't get me wrong, I've also been given some great editorial feedback which I felt made my stories stronger without alienating my characters or overall theme.

My advice to anyone who is on this path is write from the heart and trust the story. Even if you're told there's no market for your story—don't give up. There are now more opportunities to get your work to the readers. Always treat your writing like a business and do your research.

Writing for the market isn't a bad decision, just make sure it is truly the story you want to tell. It's important to know what's selling and what editors are looking for if you choose to go this route. You can't write an effective story if it's not one that you are passionate about. You must love your story more than anyone else.

Your readers will know the difference.

I've had to walk away from offers because their vision did not align with mine and while I was disappointed, I know that I made the right choice for me. Overall, I have no regrets.

Jacquelin Thomas is an award-winning, best-selling author with 93 titles published. Her books have garnered several awards, including two EMMA awards, the Romance In Color Reviewers Award, Readers Choice

Award and the Atlanta Choice Award in the Religious & Spiritual category.

Jacquelin-Thomas.com

PHAEDRA PATRICK

WHEN I THINK OF all the tough decisions I made while trying to become a published author, my biggest issue was choosing *what* to write. In a vast ocean of books and authors, how could I possibly stand out? What did agents and publishers actually want? I wrote six or seven novels trying to second guess this ... and failing miserably. I felt like I needed a crystal ball to succeed. But of course, there wasn't one.

Things only changed when I decided to write something for myself, rather than trying to predict the marketplace. I told the critical voice in my head to shut up and I let my imagination flow without questioning it. The result was a novel that came straight from my heart, and I think others recognised that.

My advice is to never criticise or compare yourself to others, because each of us is unique. And that uniqueness is what you should tap into with your writing. Do you have a prized possession? What drives you or makes you get out of bed in the morning? Do you have an unusual hobby or job? What makes you laugh or cry? Because your own differences could be the key to making your book stand out. If you tell a story with passion, it will shine through and prove compelling to others, too.

Phaedra Patrick's books have been translated into twenty-five languages worldwide and her first three

novels were all *USA Today* bestsellers. Her second novel *Rise and Shine Benedict Stone* has been made into a Hallmark movie.

Phaedra-Patrick.com

H. D. THOMSON

WHEN I FIRST STARTED out, I wrote for the love of it. I didn't focus on the market. It wasn't in my vocabulary. Over time, I had author friends tell me to write to the market; otherwise, I wasn't going to get anywhere in the industry. I disliked the idea. I wanted to write something different than what was out there, be that fresh voice that readers talked about. I continued to write, learning the craft, but getting rejection after rejection. If I didn't get form letters, I would receive letters that expounded on my strong writing skills, along with the standard phrase 'it's not for us.'

After a truckload of rejections (I lost track of how many. Probably close to a hundred), I started to write for the market. I soon published with small presses, not really liking what I was writing, but hey, I was published. Over time I lost the joy of creating stories. I began to hate the whole publishing industry.

I stopped writing. The idea of it turned my stomach.

Like in life, there are times when you need to let go and trust yourself and the universe or God. It took me forever to realize that. I wanted to get published with a New York publisher so bad that I could taste it, feel it, but it wasn't happening, which fed my frustration. I think that fear of not becoming the 'successful' author I had envisioned, with all the limitations I had put with it, pushed my dreams of being a writer from my grasp. The need to create with words withered to the point where I disliked everything about writing and the industry.

After several years of turning my back on writing, stories began whispering inside my head. The 'what if' scenarios would start distracting me. Eventually, they won, and I started to write again. Instead of going the New York publishing route, I got my rights back from the books I had previously published with small presses and self-published my previously rejected books. They're all well-reviewed and 'different' than the norm, and that's fine with me. Readers do seem to like them, and ultimately their opinion is what really matters.

I'm back to loving the writing process again. I'd boxed myself into what I considered a successful writer 'should be,' and because of it, closed doors and opportunities. I lost sight of why I started writing in the first place.

I learned that you have to be careful. If you enjoy the genre you're writing or the subject line, you'll be fine. It's when you write to a market you dislike, push yourself with deadlines, and completely constrict your creativity that you get into dangerous territory. Following such a path, you'll discover the joy of writing is sucked out of you. I've seen many an author give up a successful career because they lost their love for writing.

Don't lose that joy of creating words, characters, and stories. Because once you do, writing becomes one of 'those' jobs you're trying to escape from.

H.D. Thomson, two-time Romance Writers of America Golden Heart finalist, winner of the Emily in paranormal romance, and paranormal romance finalist in the Suzannah. H.D. loves writing about tortured heroes and heroines and ordinary people placed in extraordinary circumstances.

HDThomson.com

PHILLIP MARGOLIN

WHEN I TALK TO writing groups, I tell them to never think of writing as a career because it is very hard to get published, and most published writers don't earn enough to live on. The good news is that while you can't be a writer and do brain surgery or try murder cases as a hobby, you can be a doctor, plumber or teacher and write as a hobby. Always write because you love writing. If you write something good enough for publication and you can earn enough to support yourself that's great, but the writing alone should be the motivation. I also tell these groups to think and not write when they get an idea. I have spent years between getting an idea and writing when I could not think of a great ending. Don't rush. If you don't have a contract, you don't have a deadline.. Develop your plot and characters in your head, then write an outline when you know your ending. While you work on your outline, you are thinking and not writing and you get more and more ideas. When the outline is done, your book is written and you just have to flesh it out.

Phillip Margolin, award-winning author, with over 28 bestselling novels in print, and author of *The Last Innocent Man* and *Gone, But Not Forgotten*(novel), both of which were made into films. Philip also was the president of Chess for Success, a non-profit organization that is dedicated to helping children develop skills

necessary for success in school, and still volunteers as a board member.

PhillipMargolin.com

MICHELLE MAJOR

I THINK EVERY WRITER I know discovered their love of telling stories through a love of reading them. Like many avid readers, I devoured books as a kid. My mom jokes that sending me to my room wasn't a punishment because that was my happy place—curled up in my bed with my weekly library haul or—when I saved enough money—something special from the Scholastic Book Fair. I was the kid with the flashlight up way past my bedtime for just one more page. Always one more page.

I excelled at writing in school but I never considered making fiction writing a career. I had bills to pay and a life to live—journaling or dabbling in creative writing could only be a hobby. One I had little time for given everything else I had to do. But in a particularly awful position where my job was basically to fly around the country and lay off employees for my bankrupt company, I randomly picked up a romance novel in an airport bookstore. Thirty years old and I truly believed commercial fiction was beneath me. In the pages of that historical romance, I lost myself again in the best way possible. It reminded me that reading for pleasure was the best escape, and it also inspired me.

If I'd paid attention to the books I loved when I was younger and the reasons they found a place in my heart, I would have noticed a pattern. I adored the emotions of stories and particularly the romance thread. Anne and Gilbert. Elizabeth and Darcy. Jo and

Laurie (and then reluctantly Amy and Laurie). I resonated with the love story in any book I read. When I discovered the genre of romance, it changed my life. I found my voice writing love stories and through these stories of hope and healing, I wrote myself into the best career I can imagine.

The advice I'd give my younger self and any aspiring writer there is to pay attention to your heart and the stories that resonate with you as a reader. Don't think you can't write something because it's too commercial or not literary or any other restriction that the outside world might want to place on you. Write what you love because that's the best way to find your voice and to craft stories that will resonate with readers. Write what you love because this is a hard business—after over fifty books published I can say that with certainty. Loving the work is essential for doing the work. And doing the work is what makes you a writer.

Michelle Major is the *USA Today* bestselling author of over fifty sexy and sweet contemporary romances. She loves second-chances love stories, smart heroines and strong heroes. A Midwesterner at heart, she's made the Rocky Mountains her home for nearly half her life and is thrilled to share her books with readers.

MichelleMajor.com

JEREMY BATES

WHAT WOULD I HAVE told my younger self to help him get published? I can think of enough stuff to fill a book—and many authors have done just that, written a book on the topic. Which is why I think *What I Wished I'd Known* is a great concept. It's not a single author dispensing advice on his/her literary journey; it's a whopping one hundred. If you can't find some salient advice in here, you're probably not serious about writing and publishing. So what two cents can I contribute?

Let me digress for a minute and say this: I think everybody has a story inside them. The difficulty is getting it down on paper. Most people can't do that. Not for any lack of imagination. They don't try. Because—let's be honest, folks—writing is a slog. If you think about it, a fiction writer's job (aside from imagining up the plot and characters and setting) involves sitting on your ass and staring at a computer screen for five or six hours a day, trying to figure out how to arrange an absurd number of words into a pleasing, coherent structure that other people would find interesting to read. What the fuck, right? Put that way, authorship seems like a terrible pastime or profession. Of course, as with most everything in life, the harder you work, the greater the payoff. So if you're willing to sit through that slog, then I assure you that you'll find a lot of reward in crafting something that thousands or perhaps millions of strangers will ultimately want to read.

Yeah, yeah, hurry up and get to the point, Bates, you're probably thinking. *I know I want to be a writer. I know what's involved. I know the payoff's great. Why do you think I'm reading this freakin-friggin-frackin book? So stop pontificating and get to the actual advice.*

Right you are then. The first thing I would have told my younger self would be to *write in the genre you know and love, and not the one you think would be more commercially successful*. Seems like a no-brainer, yes? Well, this is probably one of the biggest mistakes aspiring writers make. I know I made it. You see, the genre I write in today is horror, and the first book I ever wrote and completed (though it was never published) was horror. However, hardly any literary agents back in the mid aughts were looking for adult horror novels. They were the black sheep in literary circles. In fact, Dorchester Publishing was really the only major publisher then that published mass market paperback horror novels, and it was on a downhill trajectory, eventually going out of business in 2010. I recall one literary agent in those days who had been openly hostile to my pitch, suggesting snidely I rebrand the book a "bizarre thriller" rather than horror.

A bizarre thriller? Really?

Anyway, my first book was published a couple of years later. It was called *White Lies*, and it was a psychological thriller. This was followed the next year by *The Taste of Fear*, an action thriller. Genre-wise, I was all over the place because I was putting idea over genre. The premise for *White Lies* (what if a woman told a white lie that spiraled out of control until her life was in jeopardy?) sounded pretty cool so I went with it. Same with *The Taste of Fear*. A wealthy American couple getting kidnapped and whisked away deep into the Congo jungle sounded straight out of the headlines of the day. The thing was, I didn't read psychological thrillers and action thrillers. I might pick one up every now and then, sure, but the stuff I liked, the stuff I grew up reading, the stuff in my blood, was horror. So writing psychological and action fiction…? I felt like the guy at the party who doesn't know anybody and is trying too hard to fit in. This is why, I believe, I found it difficult to follow up my first two books with a third one. I was unanchored, adrift. Eventually I wrote something—I'm not sure what genre I'd classify it as belonging to—but my publisher didn't want it and released me from my contract.

That's when I decided *fuck it*. I'm going to self-publish because then I can write whatever the hell I want. Naturally, I went back to the horror genre, and the book I wrote was called *Suicide Forest*. I'd had the idea in my head for a long time because I'd previously lived in Japan and had been by the forest. But I never thought it would be publishable because 1) it was horror and 2) it was set in Japan.

Upon its release back in 2014 it did far better than either of my two traditionally published books—and to this day remains one of my better selling titles. Since then I've followed it up with five more books in the series, and another five in a similar series based on real legends instead of real places.

The bottom line: I spent years writing books that weren't *me*, if you get what I mean, because I thought they were more commercially viable than the stuff I truly knew and loved. I wouldn't call those years a waste because I learned a lot about writing and so forth. However, I think if you choose to write in a genre that isn't *you*, that you don't know inside-out and upside-down, then you're going to hit a dead-end eventually. You hear all the time *write what you know*...well, what I'm getting at, I suppose, is to *write in the genre you know*.

Writing's a slog, remember? No need to make it any tougher or more frustrating than it already is.

This leads into the second thing I would have told my younger self had I a genie in a bottle willing to grant me such a wish. *Find your voice as quickly as you can and stick with it*. It shouldn't come as a surprise that by committing yourself to a genre you truly know and love will make finding your voice that much easier. In my case, writing *White Lies* and *The Taste of Fear* were the slogs of all slogs. I would have a finished draft of either manuscript, I would think it was good enough to send off to a literary agent...and then I would read a random book, be razzle-dazzled by the author's writing style (which is essentially his or her voice), and then go back to my manuscript and rework the entire thing! Then I would read another random book and be razzle-dazzled again...you can see where this is going. No voice = no confidence = a weak story = a whole lot of wasted time.

It wasn't until *Suicide Forest* that I found my own voice. Was this because I was finally writing in the genre that I knew and loved? I would be hard-pressed to argue otherwise. And I'll tell you this much, folks. Listening to the voice inside your head, and not to all the others already out there, makes the writing process much, much easier. By no longer obsessing over syntax and how the words and sentences appear on paper, you'll no longer be looking at the page but beyond it. You'll lose yourself in the story. You'll be going with the flow and all that Zen stuff. It's really the only way to write fresh and compelling fiction. It's gotta come from you, and it's gotta *be* you.

Oh—one final point of a minor nature: watch out for adverbs. In his book *On Writing*, Stephen King compared adverbs to a field of dandelions. One is pretty and special, but a lawn choked with them isn't something anybody wants. This analogy is all well and true. My addition is to call out some of the adverbs you should keep an eye open for. When I was in the early stages of my writing career, and heard about the evils of adverbs, I always thought about the ones you tack onto dialogue tags. "Don't do that," he said *urgently*. Or "Please help me," she said *desperately*. The accepted wisdom is that the reader should know by the context of the scene that the man is speaking urgently and that the woman is speaking desperately, hence you don't need to point it out with an adverb. Nevertheless, I have come to understand there are other sneaky adverbs—shadow adverbs, if you will—that don't jump out at you but can still choke and possibly kill your story. Think along the lines of "just" and "really" and "only" etc. These silent devils can creep into your writing so much so you don't even notice that you might be incorporating them every few sentences. Weeding them out (a simple CTR + F will do the trick until you train yourself to spot them instantly) can make a drastic difference to the quality of your writing. Instead of "He just wanted to go home" write "He wanted to go home"; instead of "She really needed a hug" write "She needed a hug." Your readers will thank you for it. Just trust me. ~~Just~~ Trust me.

Jeremy Bates, author of *Suicide Forest* and *The Sleep Experiment*

JeremyBatesBooks.com

NETWORKING AND THE SOLITARY WRITER

"Writing is a solitary endeavor, but not a lonely one. When you write, your world is populated by the characters you invent and you feel those people filling your lives."

— Danielle Steel

RHYS BOWEN

WHAT I WISH I'D known was nobody is going to roll out a red carpet for you. A great deal of your success as a writer lies with you. When you publish your first book, you are ecstatic and expect to see it reviewed everywhere, on every bookshelf. Not going to happen. For the average first book there will be no publicity help from the publisher (unless they have paid you a million. Then they'll work to get that back). I soon realized I'd have to win readers one at a time: so I visited every bookstore, made friends with the owners, left bookmarks. I spoke to every book group and library that invited me. I joined the right professional organizations—for me it was Mystery Writers of America and Sisters in Crime. I volunteered. I became chapter chair. I went to every convention. I also answered every fan letter and built up a mailing list. (This was back in the 1990s so before social media)

These days I work hard at social media. Readers love to feel connected to writers. But in balancing remember that writing a good book comes first! My visibility expanded when I started winning awards. Every book should be better than the one before!

Rhys Bowen is the *New York Times* bestselling author of two historical mystery series and several internationally bestselling historical stand alone novels, including *The Venice Sketchbook*. Her work has been translated

into thirty languages to date and has won twenty major awards. Rhys is a transplanted Brit who divides her time between California and Arizona.

RhysBowen.com

BENEDICT BROWN

IT'S A COMMON REFRAIN that writing is a solitary business, and I believed that to be the case for a long time. As a Brit writing in English but living in Spain, I spent about fifteen years writing books before I found a community of fellow authors to support me. Once I had, it made everything else much easier.

I started out writing children's literature but didn't find success until I changed to murder mysteries. I write fast and publish often, which means spending many hours locked away in my office, tapping at the keyboard (and occasionally laughing at my own jokes). As a result, I don't see a lot of people most days. My four-year-old daughter will normally convince me to stop what I'm doing at some point and play Lego with her but, for the most part, I'm alone, trying to get the word count up and my ideas down.

When I was at university in Britain, I looked for other authors who were motivated and serious about their writing. I did a Master's in creative writing and even ran workshops of my own, but it was not always easy to find people at the same stage of the journey as me. When I moved to Spain to be an English teacher, I never gave up on my dream, though I probably would have if it hadn't been for the friends I made through online writing groups.

Not only did I meet my most ardent supporter – a fellow writer who read every word I wrote and encouraged me whenever things looked bleak – but I gained countless opinions on my work, and I would eventually make the contact who would change my life. Just at the point at which I became a parent – and assumed I'd have to give up on the career I'd spent all that time preparing to do – I met a successful mystery writer who suggested I change genre. I have since published fifteen novels, created a six-figure career for myself and not looked back.

My interaction with other authors online has changed dramatically in that time. I'm no longer searching for people to give me feedback on my work, but I still rely on them just as much. Only fellow authors know what the career we've chosen is really like. They can sympathise with the lows and celebrate the highs of an unusual lifestyle. Through forums, Facebook groups, and writer's websites, I've found my tribe and I couldn't do the job I love without them.

Success as a writer makes things easier. I now also enjoy the regular e-mails from my readers and have built up a big ARC team which is indispensable for my editing process and for helping me improve as a writer. But it's the first steps in writing (and especially publishing) that are the hardest. I wish I'd known just how vital it is to find support during those early stages. I'm happy to say that, though I still spend most of my days alone in my office, it no longer feels so solitary.

Benedict Brown is originally from South London, but currently lives in Spain with his wife where he writes cozy mysteries. Having earned MA in Creative Writing and grew up with a crime family, he writes the Izzy Palmer Mysteries and bestselling Lord Edgington Investigates series.

BenedictBrown.net

RACHELLE BURK

WRITING IS, BY ITS nature, a solitary activity. I was convinced that my first children's stories, written during the quiet hours the kids were at school, were clever and adorable. My family, my kids' teachers, our librarian had only praise for my stories! So why did all my submissions receive form rejection letters? My confidence began to suffer.

I wish I'd known earlier that writing shouldn't be so isolating. I needed support. I needed critical, unbiased feedback. I needed a *writing community*.

Eventually I joined SCBWI (Society of Children's Book Writers & Illustrators), and attended conferences and workshops. Most importantly, I found critique groups of other children's writers. We exchange manuscripts, share critical feedback on plot, characterization, and dialogue, and brainstorm plotlines or endings that just aren't working. We learn from each other.

Our group members also keep each other motivated, and share resources, articles, and news from the writing world. Together we commiserate after rejection letters and celebrate the publishing contracts.

As I quickly learned, my early "brilliant" stories had been typically novice—overdone themes filled with stilted dialogue, cliches, and a "telling" style. But with knowledgeable feedback from my critique groups and the wider writing community, these early Terrible Stories became Mediocre Stories, then Pretty Good Stories, and finally Published Stories. I can honestly say that I would never have had a single word published without my writing groups, and my group members would all say the same. The icing on the cake is that many of these writers have become my best friends.

Whether online or in person, writer groups and communities provide feedback, support, guidance, motivation, and a sense of belonging. While there are various groups for specific genres, here are a few general resources for finding a critique group and writing community: CritiqueCircle.com, Scribophile.com, Writerscafe.org, Reddit.com/r/writing, Absolutewrite.com/forums, Inkedvoices. com.

Rachelle Burk writes both fiction and nonfiction for children ages 2-14. Her publications include picture books, chapter books, and a middle-grade novel. She has also written for *Highlights for Children* and *Scholastic Science World* magazines. Rachelle visits schools around the country with her dynamic Author Visit programs. Rachelle's award-winning website, ResourcesForChildrensWriters.com, has been included in *Writers Digest Magazine's* annual list "101 Best Websites for Writers."

RachelleBurk.Blogspot.com

JACQUELINE DRUGA

I USED TO SIT every night at my old Sears typewriter when I was ten years old, penning short stories with action heroes like Charlton Heston. No one really got my obsession with him because even at ten, he was well before my time. I'd enthusiastically finish the story and present it proudly to my mom. She would say, "It's wonderful dear, I'll read it in a little bit."

She never did.

In fact getting people close to me to read anything I wrote or write now is like asking them to drink Drano. They're reluctant and uncomfortable and put it off, hoping eventually I'd stop asking.

I did.

Maybe I am the norm, maybe I am not, but I wish when I pulled those finished pages I would have realized that people close to you, just don't care. I mean they do, but they don't care enough to read. As if what I write can't possibly be as good as a Michael Crichton book, because, well, they know me. Even as I gained success no one was every curious enough to read a page.

I am envious when I hear other writers talk about how their parents and family read everything they write. That wasn't the case with me. My disappointment over unread material left with me with self doubt as to the quality of my writing.

I wish I would have known then not to expect or count on support and encouragement from those nearest to me. That they didn't nor would they get it. I had to be my own biggest drive and fan to continue on, I would have stopped asking them to read long before I did.

Jacqueline Druga, prolific writer and filmmaker, who favors post-apocalypse and apocalypse writing. Currently, many of her films can be found on Amazon Prime and YouTube.

JacquelineDruga.com

HARD TRUTHS

"Writing a book is a horrible, exhausting struggle, like a long bout of some painful illness. One would never undertake such a thing if one were not driven on by some demon whom one can neither resist nor understand."

— George Orwell, Why I Write

GINJER L CLARKE

I WISH I HAD known that the work of a children's author would always be undervalued economically. This knowledge wouldn't have changed my desire to be published and to share the weird, wonderful world of nonfiction science with young readers. But it might have made me fight harder early on for the appropriate value of my work. Many people are so focused on being published and grateful to the publishers who make that dream happen that they accept any compensation offered. I have certainly negotiated significant rate increases since my first publishing contracts more than 20 years ago, but it's always difficult to overcome that starting point. I wish that publishers valued creative work as much as profits, but that also requires consumers to be willing to pay an appropriate cost for the art beyond just the material costs.

Undervaluing is also true regarding a children's author's time and knowledge. I wish I had known that everyone (and their mother!) would want to publish a children's book and assume that you can help them do so—for free. I don't know of another occupation where those who have achieved success are so regularly asked to give away their secrets, offer their connections, and provide unlimited advice. I have certainly done these things many times over the years. Sometimes I am compensated for conference talks, manuscript critiques, and editorial suggestions. But more often I get cornered at parties, direct messaged in all forms of social media, approached during exercise classes, and once even at a doctor's appointment! I love helping other writers understand the craft and business of children's publishing. But there seem to be no boundaries to these requests and no understanding of limits to the time and knowledge that can be freely given before there is no time left to create income-producing work. I wish others would please value the achievements of those who have made a career as children's authors and illustrators before assuming that the keys to this success are easily conveyed in a short conversation or text exchange and unworthy of your monetary contribution.

I also wish that I and others had known that the economic value of writing children's books is so low that even most published authors still have side gigs. I had no idea that providing author visits at elementary schools—presentations that talk about how I got started writing, how a book is made, and discuss topics such as research and revision, while including fun facts and humorous anecdotes—would be the main source of my income. I truly love this part of my job, and fortunately I have a background in theatre performance that translated well. But it's fascinating to see that teachers often yearn to be authors and to do what I do, unaware that the income from book royalties is so variable, unknown, and infrequent that presenting in schools is the mainstay of my income. And I still make less than teachers most years!

I am grateful. I love my job, both the writing and presenting parts. It's a unique career that allows me to be self-employed, self-motivated, and self-directed. I follow my passions and spend most of my time doing my favorite things: reading, learning, and writing. In fact, having to do only virtual school programs for the last two years during the pandemic has made me so anxious to return to schools in-person soon. I can't wait to once again cherish the connections made with young readers, the information imparted, and the joy of sharing my passion for reading, writing, and weird science. Many students think authors and illustrators are rockstars. They ask: "Are you famous? Are you rich?" Because *they* truly value the books we create. If only the adults did fully, too. The truth is that I get paid in hugs, thank-you letters, and the knowledge that my books help young kids to be more confident readers, to be more curious about their world, and to be interested in the concept of how ideas become books.

I want you to have these joys, too. I want you to experience the immense satisfaction of holding your published book in your hands and then seeing it in the hands of young readers. But I want you to know first that even though a career in children's publishing is possible, the skills required to achieve it are so grossly undervalued (especially for a nonfiction author and especially for a female author, but those are issues for another day) that you will probably be low paid, have to create other income streams, and still be expected to give away your time. Most days, all of that is more than worth it when a student tells me, "I want to be an author, too!" May it be so for you as well.

Ginjer L. Clarke writes fun, fact-filled nonfiction books about weird, wonderful science stuff, including most recently *Are Sea Monsters Real?* and *Tiny Terrors! The World's Scariest Small Creatures*. She is the author of more than 30 picture books, beginning readers, and chapter books, with many more exciting titles on the way. Ginjer lives in Richmond, Virginia, and is available for energetic, educational, and engaging K-6 school visits both in-person and online.

GinjerClarkeBooks.com
Facebook/Instagram/Twitter: @GinjerClarkeBooks

JENNIFER ASHLEY

WHAT I WISH I'D known is perhaps a little different from what others might say. I wish I had understood what a physical, mental, and emotional toll being a full-time author can take.

We don't notice when we're sitting and typing all day—whether drafting a novel, or revising or proofreading it, or doing marketing—how long we've been stationary and what a physical drain it can be. I hear constantly about authors who have had to cease writing for months to years because they burned themselves out, physically and emotionally. We are pushed to write more, more, more, faster and faster. This can be very stressful and draining, and we try to keep running until we hit a wall.

At one point a few years ago, after I turned in a manuscript, I feared I might not be able to write another book. Not because I couldn't think of stories, or because my words had dried up. The stories were there in my head and continued to dance around in my brain.

But I was in so much physical pain that the thought of sitting down at the keyboard made me want to cry. What I didn't understand is that though we are not doing physical labor, writing actually is physically demanding, but this is a difficult concept to grasp. It isn't coal mining or nursing or other high-intensity jobs, but the stress on your arms and back, not to mention your mental health, can deplete you.

I knew something had to give. I decided to look at my habits and find a way to fix myself. I evaluated how much I moved (or didn't), what I ate, and went to a doctor to figure out my overall state of health. What the tests showed scared me, and I decided then and there to turn things around.

While what I did to help myself worked for *me* (eating far more healthily and hiring a physical therapist / fitness coach who designed exercises for my body and my ability, which I have been doing every week for years now), the methods of staying fit enough to write will vary for each person. We are all in different stages of physical health and age, have different genetics, different environments, different demands on our time, etc. What I did might not work for others, and what they do might not have worked for me.

The point was for me to assess what was wrong and tackle the problem instead of deciding to give up my career.

I learned that I could not just dive into my writing and not come out, working many hours a day. I am not the only author who has discovered this, and I have seen more seminars now on working less—using the "work smarter not harder" adage.

It really doesn't matter the author's level of success: whether she's a mega bestseller or selling a modest number of books to a niche audience. Either career path is completely valid, but both require the same amount of physical writing work and mental stress. Acknowledging that and introducing healthy work habits (e.g., not sitting on at a desk for eight hours at a time, putting movement into our lives, and making sure that we're not staying up all night eating candy to keep us going) keeps an author from crashing and burning—and burnout can be bad. You might not be able to write at all after that.

Now, my journey will be different from others'. My physical health turned around once I added healthy food, exercise, meditation, and rest. I know authors who are struggling with far more complicated health issues, but my point is, writing is an added stress and strain on top of everything else we juggle. We need to balance our careers and our health.

So that's what the biggest thing I wished I'd known before I started. I've learned a lot about marketing and the publishing business during this journey, but now I wish I'd known how not to drain myself trying to write too many books and keep up with the industry.

We *can* keep up, and have a career, without endangering our health beyond the point of no return, but we have to first acknowledge that writing can be a physical and emotional strain and address that issue.

Jennifer Ashley is a *New York Times* and *USA Today* bestselling author who writes historical, paranormal, and contemporary romance; mysteries as Ashley Gardner; and paranormal romance and urban fantasy as Allyson James.

JenniferAshley.com

ANGUS DONALD

THERE IS A THOUGHT-EXPERIMENT I have often found useful when trying to decide whether something is worth doing. I imagine I have £10 million in the bank and ask myself how that would affect my decision? I would urge anyone contemplating a career as a fiction author to have a crack at this. If you would still embark on a writing career as a rich man or woman – fantastic! You probably have the makings of a fine wordsmith (and you can afford to pay handsomely to market your work). But, if you think you are going to earn £10 million as an author of fiction, if you think you might actually be the next J. K. Rowling, you would be wise to think again.

"No man but a blockhead ever wrote except for money," said Dr Samuel Johnson. I disagree. There are hundreds of thousands, if not millions, of perfectly intelligent people out there right now who are writing their novels – I read recently that since the advent of self-publishing on Amazon and other ebook platforms, there are 400,000 novels published *every year* in the USA – and most of these people are doing it out of sheer love for their literary craft. The blockheads among them are bashing away at their keyboards because they truly believe they'll scoop up a fortune by their efforts.

I was one of those blockheads. I genuinely thought twenty years ago, when I started trying to write historical fiction, that I would get rich from it – that it was only a matter of time before money cascaded from the heavens. How wrong I was. I've just about managed to scrape a living since my first novel – the bestselling *Outlaw*, first in my long-running Robin Hood series – was published in 2009. My family has not starved – yet – and we somehow manage to pay the bills, but it has not been easy by any means. If I could go back in time, I would say: "For God's sake, Angus, do not quit your well-paid day job!" This advice still holds good for all aspiring authors.

It is not that people don't read any more, they still do, despite myriad other forms of entertainment being available, from three-D video games to a cornucopia of excellent streaming TV, it's just there is so much competition from other books. Publishers want "sure things" these days – they are increasingly reluctant to take a chance on a new author, without a proven track record. The book charts are filled each week with familiar names, the same authors appearing again and again. I have discovered that the main thing that distinguishes a well-written book that is a mad, runaway success, and one that is equally fine, is the amount of money spent on marketing, promoting and advertising it. The big publishers, when they get behind a new book, can almost guarantee it becomes a bestseller. But what they want is another book from Richard Osman, James Patterson or Danielle Steel. A sure thing. Not your unknown novel, no matter how brilliant it may be. Smaller publishers may take the risk on your exciting new work but they will also demand that the author to do much of the marketing and advertising heavy lifting on social media – and possibly even spend his or her own money pushing the book – and, with self-publishing, now a respectable option, the marketing, and thereby success of a book, is *all* down to the author's own efforts. This is where having that £10 mill comes in handy! You will need to splash it about.

If you are not already a big name, or rich, you will travel a much rougher road. And the odds against making living with your pen, or becoming even slightly better off, are stacked against you. But if you actually love writing for its own sake, you're not going to let *that* stop you. Forge ahead! Get your bum in that seat and start tapping away! If writing truly is its own reward, you don't need a financial one, despite what that nincompoop Dr Johnson may have said. On the other hand, if you *don't* enjoy the actual writing process – or that warm, sustaining, "having written something half-decent" feeling – then maybe, just maybe, the threadbare literary life is not for you.

Angus Donald is the bestselling author of sixteen historical fiction novels and one fantasy tome. His latest series begins with The Last Berserker (Fire Born 1), an epic Viking saga, which is available from Amazon and other booksellers. He is always delighted to chat about his books to readers on his website – www.angusdonaldbooks.com – or on Twitter or FaceBook.

SHARON SALA

I WAS ALWAYS A dreamer. I was always a storyteller. Those two things were innate within me, but becoming a writer was like walking into another universe - into a world I didn't know, with language unknown to me, and rules that didn't always seem fair.

Things I wish I'd known from the onset seem simple now, but when first faced with them, they were either surprising, shocking, or self-defeating.

Of all the things you must become as a writer, the first thing outside of telling a good story is first to believe in yourself, and second, to grow your own body armor.

- I wish I'd known about AAR. The Association of Author Representatives. Never pick a literary agent who does not belong to this association.

- I wish I'd known that valid agents aren't allowed to charge reading fees, either for prospective clients, or for clients already within their agency.

- I wish I'd known that the beloved publisher who bought my first book may cease to exist without notice, or absorbed into another publishing house.

- I wish I'd been prepared for the editor/writer relationship required of a published author. It's like dating. Some are nightmares, and some of them are winners.

- I also wish I'd known about the internal shakeups within a publishing house that would also impact me. Like writing for a line that is dropped without notice. Or having a wonderful editor one day, and finding out they'd moved on, or been let go. It's like a death in the family.

- I wish I'd known that sometimes a publisher not only drops the editor, but the writers they worked with, as well.

- I wish I'd known sooner that if you don't get it in writing in a contract you're going to sign, you cannot assume the 'promises' of a publishing house will come to fruition.

- I wish I'd known sooner that publishers only want writers to stay in one genre, and that when that genre suddenly falls out of style, instead of freeing them to move into another genre for the same publisher, they just dump the writers and get new ones, for less money, to write the latest genres in fashion.

The writing is always on the wall. But it's hard to see it for the spin of being published, and doing what you always dreamed of doing.

So very few ever become the darlings.

So very few ever hit the big lists.

And it's not because of lack of talent.

It's just who the publishers choose to promote.

I wish I'd known this sooner. It would have saved a lot of anger and disappointment.

And I wish I'd known sooner how truly powerful I can be on my own. That my worth is not measured by someone else's opinion. That I can be who I need to be. Write what I want to write.

It's harder to make a living at it.

But I wish I'd known sooner that I have something of worth to share with the world.

Stories.

My stories.

They will live on long after I am gone.

Sharon Sala has over 135 books and novellas in print, published in six different genres – romance, young adult, western, fiction, and women's fiction and non-fiction. First published in 1991, she's an eight-time RITA finalist, winner of the Janet Dailey Award, five-time Career Achievement winner from RT Magazine, five time winner of the National Reader's Choice Award, and five time

winner of the Colorado Romance Writer's Award of Excellence, winner of the Heart of Excellence Award, as well as winner of the Booksellers Best Award.

SharonSala.com

LYNN CAHOON

I WISHED I'D KNOWN that my words weren't precious. That once the story was sold, the publisher, the editor, and sometimes even your agent, has a say in what gets published. I held on to 'my' story for too long before I realized the basic fact of writing. If you want to be published, you're selling your story. Which means you're inviting people into your world. From your publishing team to the readers who want to explain why your character would have done something differently, they all want to mess with your story. So the lesson is to figure out when a critique or a suggestion makes the story better and when it doesn't. Get a good team around you and trust them. Then trust your heart when you disagree.

Lynn Cahoon, *New York Times* and *USA Today* bestselling author -of six cozy series - Making cozy communities one book, one series, at a time. A place where you want to live and grow with a cast of characters who feel more like the family you'd create for yourself.

LynnCahoon.com

DONNA EVERHART

YOU'VE MADE IT. YOUR agent has secured a book deal and you are certain from this point on your stories will always grace the shelves of bookstores. Without a doubt getting published is hard, but, did you know *staying* published is even harder? I didn't. When I first heard this, I was stunned. What do you mean? It took years to get here! I want to *stay*. We go into our writing careers with the singular goal of publication. Once there, we imagine our work is guaranteed to be put out into the world. Sadly, this is not always true and there isn't a lot about this a writer can control – except one thing. More on that in a bit.

First of all, I'm beyond grateful I've been able to remain under contract. However, at this moment, I can think of a half dozen author friends who were published at one point, and who don't currently have a new contract. They are very fine writers, every one of them. Talented, and savvy, they once had the enviable book contracts, they had "made it," so, how does this happen?

Each of their paths is uniquely different, so, there isn't a singular crisp answer, but usually the biggest reason is **book sales**. Depending on the publisher, if a book sells 25,000 copies, it's considered to have done excellent. A book selling about 15,000 copies is oftentimes strong enough for a publisher to consider another contract. It's true the industry is aware of the "sophomore slump," meaning a second book typically doesn't do as well as the first. The fact the industry has a name for it means they get it, they understand this happens. After that, however, book sales ought to be in the black, not red.

Another reason is **competition**. The numbers are staggering for how many novels come out each month, and there's your little book trying to scrape its way to the top of the heap, and get its due share of attention. Some of this can be driven by the work of the publicist, but it's the story, too.

Another unforeseen, or unexpected factor is **writing the book no one wants**, or, a book that's **not a fit for the current market**. It happens. It's a precarious perch a published author inhabits. We like to explore, and try new ideas. Sometimes the idea works, sometimes it doesn't. It's really hard to let go of a project you've spent a long time with, but it's the best thing you can do for yourself. Moving on will renew your hope, re-energize your creativity, and get you away from the negative association that goes along with a project that didn't make it.

How does one *stay published* in such a volatile industry? It's not helpful to say there are no guarantees, but this is the truth. I also believe there are second chances. Consider another author acquaintance I know whose debut came out several years ago, and did well. This author wrote another book and no one was interested, including the publisher of the first book. Several years later, when the publishing world had all but forgotten about this writer, out of the blue came a deal with one of the top five publishers. This writer was back in the game again.

As to the others I mentioned, what do you think they're doing?

They're *writing*. If you suddenly, and surprisingly find yourself without book deal, you might think it's the end of your career as an author. It's not, or it doesn't have to be, because the part you *can* control is to keep writing.

Donna Everhart is the *USA Today* bestselling author of Southern fiction with authenticity and grit, including the Southeastern Library Association Award-winning *The Road to Bittersweet* and her most recent novel, *The Moonshiner's Daughter*. Her fifth novel, The Saints of Swallow Hill, is out now.

DonnaEverhart.com

MICHAEL J. TOUGIAS

THIRTY-EIGHT YEARS OF writing and 30 books for adults and 8 for young adults makes me a "veteran." I've had NY *Times* bestsellers with Simon & Schuster and books with miniscule sales with small publishers. Along the way, I made plenty of mistakes, but can also look back and see what I did right. Which leads me to these key practices listed below that every writer should learn. I'm hoping some of these tips make your journey a bit smoother than mine and you find joy in the process and success in your bank account!

Try for an Agent

Agents can open doors to the large publishers that are closed to non-agented writers. Why go with a large publisher? They have the clout to have your book reviewed by large newspapers, review magazines, etc. And they can cast the broadest of distribution possibilities from Costco to CVS Pharmacies. If you can't land an agent, don't despair, you might be able to find a quality publisher on your own. I've done both. But having a quality agent is worth every penny of their 15% of your royalties.

One bit of warning about agents, however, is that anyone can be an agent. Consequently some are fantastic and others are near useless. And if you do land an agent, insist that you get copies of the complete royalty statements from the publisher. Not all agents are honest...I learned that the hard way.

Practice Public Speaking

The opportunities for both paid and unpaid speaking gigs are limitless. From small libraries to large business groups. I estimate I've given over two thousand presentations, and sold untold numbers of books direct to the audience at the book signing after my talk. What? You say you are not comfortable in front of crowds? Fix that problem by taking a public speaking course where you practice in front of others who have the same fear as you. It's quite possible you will go from avoiding public speaking to loving it. And when you do get speaking gigs, don't pontificate, but rather be yourself, use power point visuals, and tell the story in a your book delivered in a way that makes the audience think *I gotta buy that book for myself or as a gift. Might as well do it now while the author can personalize it.*

Fiction vs Non-fiction

Most aspiring writers I meet want to write fiction because it's more fun....and that's true. But non-fiction might be a better path for your first book. With non-fiction it is possible to land a contract from a reputable publisher solely on the basis of your proposal and four sample chapters. With fiction, however, publishers generally want to see the finished product. I've done both fiction and non-fiction, and I must admit I like the fact that I can deliver and develop two or three non-fiction projects to circulate among publishers in the same time it would take me to do one fiction project. The reason is that with non-fiction I only need to complete three sample chapters to have editors review the project. I therefore increase my odds of being published: three non-fiction projects under review vs one fiction project.

Finding the Time to Write

All of us have the same number of hours in the day. Why is it some people can complete a book project while others give up because of lack of time? The answer lies in the power of saying "no." This secret has been so important to my success I wrote a book about it, titled *No Will Set You Free*. This self-help inspirational book is all about setting boundaries and utilizing your free time the *way you want*, and not letting other people or things gobble up your free time. In the beginning of this book I discuss my journey as follows:

> *When I was in my early thirties, I knew I wanted to be an author. But I had children, a mortgage, and a secure job as a manager in the insurance industry. I couldn't just quit my job and begin writing, hoping that the money would follow. I worked long hours in my management position and much of the weekends were devoted to spending time with my family. So how was I to become an author and still be a father, husband, and manager? The answer was to say no to almost everything else other than the day job and family. It would be difficult, but I thought the payoff would be worth the sacrifice.*

> *I'd been writing articles for magazines and newspapers, and I had a pretty clear idea of the time commitment that would go into writing a book. I estimated that it would take me at least a year of "moonlighting" to complete the first few chapters of the book I had in mind. And beyond the typical moonlighting — where I worked bleary-eyed on the project well into the night after the kids had gone to bed—I'd need*

to carve out other time. I made an internal vow that I'd say yes to time with my wife, kids, corporate job, and exercise, and no to most everything else for a one-year period and see if I had enough research and writing done to land a book contract. And so I began saying no to restaurant dinners, no to most parties unless my wife really wanted to go, no to weekend golfing with buddies, no to reading the newspaper, no to television, no to arguing, and no to people that drone on and on, etc.

I cannot stress enough how important time management is for aspiring authors and writers, and that the key to managing your time is by saying no to "time-suckers." Sure, I missed some fun, but I achieved my goal of writing the book, landing a contract, and the process changed my life. In fact many years later I was able to quit my corporate job entirely and make a good living as a full time author. Looking back at those years, I realize it was as much discipline and the power of little steps as it was talent that launched my career.

Saying no is so much easier if you have a particular goal or mission that you want to devote free time to. Ask yourself, *what would I want to accomplish or change if I only had more free time?* Your answer will set you free.

Procrastination and Perfectionism

A common refrain I hear from aspiring writers is that they started writing a book but gave up. When I question further, those writers mention procrastination. But when I dig even deeper they usually say something like "I couldn't get past the first page or two, the writing just wasn't where it should be." My answer is always the same "It doesn't have to be perfect. Just get it going and keep it flowing, and then go back and make it as good as you can. It's likely never going to be perfect in your mind, but it will improve as you work on it."

Don't let perfectionism lead to procrastination. Sit down, start the process. Soon you will have paragraphs completed, then an entire chapter. There will be time enough to improve your writing, as you re-read your work with a fresh eye. You can do it. Quit making excuses. And give yourself a pat on the back for every little step you make. Celebrate the smallest of achievements, and someday you will be celebrating big ones.

Michael J. Tougias is a *NY Times* bestselling author and accomplished speaker. His 30 non-fiction books include *The Finest Hours* (now a Disney movie), *A Storm Too Soon, Extreme Survival,* and *No Will Set You Free.*

MichaelTougias.com

SELF-DOUBT

"The worst enemy to creativity is self-doubt."

— Sylvia Plath

MARCI BOLDEN

ONE OF THE BIGGEST lessons I had to learn when I started publishing was to stop comparing my career to everyone else.

"I was published first. Why is her book doing better than mine?"

"I'm a great writer, too. Why did she land an agent and I didn't?"

"Why am I not as successful when I work just as hard as she does?"

Don't judge me. You've had these thoughts, too. This is natural. This is how our little brains work. We are programmed from a very young age to try to be the first, the fastest, the best, the smartest, and a hundred other things. We learn to see everything as a competition. Including our careers.

For some people, this can be a huge motivator, but for most of us, this mentality is a breeding ground for misery. And anger. And all-consuming bitterness. This kind of jealousy sure didn't do me any favors when I was first starting down this path. In fact, it undermined everything I was trying to accomplish because once the jealousy eased, I was left with a head filled with ugly self-talk chastising me for being so petty.

Yes, you know that voice too. It's another one we all have, whether we want it or not.

However, once I took the time to unpack what was really going on with all those insecure statements, I was able to recognize that my jealousy wasn't because someone else didn't deserve to have those things, but because of this unrealistic fear that there wouldn't be any success left for me if everyone else got theirs first. I had to step back and force myself to see the big picture instead of focusing on my little piece of it. We are all sitting at the same table and there really is enough for everyone. There are enough readers, there are enough books to be published, and there is definitely enough success to go around.

I wasn't being left behind. Neither are you.

Until you break this mindset, you'll never feel successful. No matter how many books you sell, there will always be someone selling more, hitting more bestseller lists, and having more book releases than you.

If you believe that your career isn't as good as someone else's, you will make yourself so unhappy that when you do reach your goals, you'll discount them because there will always be someone doing more. You will always find a way to convince yourself that you aren't trying hard enough, writing good enough, or that *you*, in all your beautiful glory, are not enough.

So how do we stop feeling like this when our entire lives have taught us to be the best?

When you see an author get a publishing deal and that ugly voice in your head starts berating you or your fellow author, you have to take a breath and step back. Have your moment of jealousy and depression, but then make a list of all that you have accomplished and pat yourself on the back for those amazing things you've done.

Acknowledge that you are jealous for what your peer has achieved, but also acknowledge that the reason you feel that way is because you'd like to have that achievement, too. After your initial knee-jerk "I could do that if only…" moment, take the time to reach out and congratulate her on her success, maybe even say, "I'd love to accomplish this, too." Then you could even follow up with, "May I reach out to you with a few questions about how you achieved this?"

The jealousy you feel when you see others winning should be fuel for you to keep going, not a reason for you to quit, and *definitely* not a reason to discount someone else's hard work.

Listen, publishing is one hell of a way to make a living. So much is out of our hands. Publishing deals don't guarantee success. Marketing doesn't guarantee success. Dancing naked under the moon and sacrificing Stephen King novels to the writer gods? Nope. That doesn't guarantee success either.

Sadly, neither does hard work and great books. That feeling of success depends on how *you* define success and which achievements *you* choose to recognize. You, and only you, can decide what makes you feel successful.

Everyone needs to have big dreams, but even big dreams have to be reached in baby steps. So, sit down right now and set three "baby step" goals. How many words are you going to write this week? How many new followers do you need to hit 500, 1000, or even 50? What online course should you take to learn about copywriting, editing, or marketing?

Write those down and reward yourself when you hit them. Every step counts. Every achievement matters. Every small goal takes you closer to those big dreams. Don't discount those steps because you think someone else is getting where you want to be faster.

But most importantly, don't forget to validate your own dang self.

"Yes! I sold 50 books this month!"

"Look at this! I have 200 followers!"

"I can't believe I wrote 500 words this week!"

Now, go buy yourself something nice. You've earned it.

Marci Bolden, author consultant and women's fiction and romance author.

MarciBolden.com

ANGELA MARSONS

WHENEVER I'M ASKED WHAT one thing I'd share with a new writer I always answer that there's no one thing but at least a couple of things I like to share. The first, in relation to writing, is to never show your first draft to anyone until you've finished it. First draft of any work is the author's chance to bond with the story and characters. I call it my sandpit and I don't let anyone else into it until the story is firmly seeded in my mind. Just one word from a reader can change your whole outlook on the journey you had in your mind.

Secondly, in relation to publishing, always remember what you fell in love with in the first place. Once you start submitting it can be a hard and long process full of rejection, self-doubt and hopelessness. It's important to separate those feelings and to keep in touch with the reasons that prompted you to pick up a pen/keyboard in the first place. If a piece of work meets no takers after exhausting all avenues put it aside and start on the next. Everything we write is practice and nothing is wasted.

It's important to remember that editors/agents/publishers aren't always right. My first crime novel was submitted to every publisher and was rejected by every single one. That one book has now sold over 1 million copies so it's important to keep the faith in your own writing and strive to improve with everything you write.

Angela Marsons is the *Wall Street Journal* and *USA Today* bestselling author of the DI Kim Stone series and her books have sold more than 5 million in 7 years.

AngelaMarsons-Books.com

TIM WAGGONER

I STARTED WRITING SERIOUSLY, with the goal of making it my life's work, when I was eighteen. I'm nearly sixty now, and as you might imagine, I've learned a few things about writing and publishing in that time, more than I could ever discuss in a short article. But if I had to choose the absolute best advice I have to pass on to newer writers, it would consist of the following items. So without further fanfare, here they are – Tim's Top Five Writing Life Lessons.

Don't buy into society's – or other writers' – paradigm for success. In America, people are what they do, and their success is judged by how many things they can acquire with the money they make. Writers often believe that the ultimate expression of a writing career is to be able to write full time and support yourself financially solely with your writing. That's when a writer has "made it." But I've known many writers who write full time and are barely living above the poverty line. Plus, they have no healthcare. They are so stressed by trying to pay bills and so worried about getting sick or injured, that they don't produce any more work than writers with day jobs. Stress is the enemy of creativity. Feeling like you have to live up to some imaginary standard that others have created – and feeling that you're constantly failing to reach that standard – can make you feel like you're a failure before you even begin. Each of us makes our own path as a writer, and it's fine if your path is different than anyone else's. In fact, it *should* be different. It's *yours*, not anyone else's. Do what you need to do to be able to make a life that's conducive to writing, whatever that means for you. I decided a long time ago that what I wanted wasn't to become rich or win a ton of awards or have millions of readers. I couldn't control whether or not I got any of these things. I decided I wanted to have a life in writing. That aim was entirely within my control, and I've achieved it. I won't know the ultimate shape that life has taken until right before I die, but there's no doubt I've created it.

It's okay to have a small audience. Writers are often told – either directly or implicitly – that they need to have the biggest audience possible. We need as many followers on social media as we can gather, as many subscribers to our newsletters as possible, as many reviews as we can get on Amazon, as many book sales, and on and on. If your goal is to make a ton of money, then all of this is true. But if you want to make money, why did you choose to become an artist in the first place? If you want to make money, go to law school or medical school. Writers pursue art because it's what we love, it's who we are, we can't imagine living life without doing it, and it makes the world a better place. If you're writing what you love and feel satisfied with your work, then it's fine if you have a small audience. If you cook a meal, how many people do you need to serve it to in order to feel satisfied? Bigger is better is a fallacy created by American consumer culture. *Better* is better, and you decide what's best for you.

Rejection means nothing more than a no from one person at one time. Rejections – from editors and agents – are the most common part of a writer's life. They are inevitable and, when you're starting out, they're numerable. They begin to add up fast, and they have a cumulative effect. They seem like a chorus of voices saying your work sucks, you suck, and you should never write again. Now it's true that at the start of a career, when a writer is still learning his or her craft, that the stories they produce may not be publishable yet. But if you keep writing and growing as an artist – and you get better at targeting your submissions to specific publications/publishers – you'll start selling. The rejections will still come, though, (I still get them sometimes) and you have to remember that unless you get specific feedback that helps provide insight on how to improve your writing – which editors and agents are under no obligation to give you – one rejection is not an all-encompassing statement about you and your writing. It's just a no. Do your best to put it behind you, keep sending your work out, and keep growing as a writer.

Building a writing career is a long haul. Sometimes *really* long. If you go immediately to self-publishing, it will hardly take any time at all – at least to get started. How long it may take you to get your work noticed and build your audience is another matter entirely. In the case of traditional publishing, the amount of time I've heard most often from people – and which my experience bears out – is that it takes about ten years. And that's just to get to the point where you're regularly selling your work. How much longer does it take to become a "success"? The rest of your life. In any art form, there is always more to learn, more to explore, more to achieve, both creatively and in terms of the business aspect. The truth is no artist probably ever reaches whatever they consider to be ultimate success. Stephen King craves acceptance from the literary establishment. Literary writers want a larger audience and more money. Writers of entertainment-based fiction covet awards for literary excellence. Dissatisfaction and restlessness are important fuel to an artist. They might even be two of the defining qualities of an artist.

Take your writing as far as you can. This advice was given to me by Pam Doyle, the teaching assistant who taught the composition class I took as a freshman in college, way back in 1983. During our final student-teacher conference, Pam said, "I urge you to take your writing as far as you can." This advice is perfect for writers. It's open-ended, doesn't focus on a single goal, and doesn't have a time limit. All of us can take our writing as far as we can, however far that may be. It makes for an achievable and mentally healthy definition of success as a writer, and because of this, it's the one piece of advice I always make sure to pass on to beginning writers.

Bonus Tip! Eric Maisel is a psychologist and author who specializes in helping creative people. He's written numerous books that can help creatives deal with the challenges of living an artistic life. You can find his books listed on his website at www.EricMaisel.com.

Tim Waggoner, winner of the Bram Stoker Award and finalist for the Shirley Jackson Award, has published close to fifty novels and seven collections of short stories since. He writes original fantasy and horror, as well as media tie-ins. He's written tie-in fiction for Supernatural, Alien, Grimm, the X-Files, Doctor Who, A Nightmare on Elm Street, and Transformers, among others. Tim is also a full-time tenured professor who teaches creative writing and composition at Sinclair College.

Facebook.com/Tim.Waggoner.9

D.L. WOOD

I HAVE ALWAYS LOVED bookstores and libraries. For as long as I can remember, I wanted to be a part of them. To find my name in a catalog, stroll over to *that* shelf, and drag my finger down the spines until reaching the books I authored. That dream coming true has been one of the great gifts of my life.

As an indie author who has been publishing for seven years now, there are a lot of things I wish I had known when I started, and I learn more of what I don't know every day. One of the most critical things I wish I'd known is how important it is to not judge myself by the experiences of other authors.

Every writer's journey is unique and there are dozens of factors that play into determining what that journey will look like. Perhaps the most important factor is the answer to the question: What is your goal? Meaning, what do you truly hope to accomplish with your writing?

It's easy to look at someone who appears to be doing the same things you are doing and critically compare yourself to their seemingly more successful experience. However, gauging your success by another author's success is a dangerous road to go down, because you are not them and they are not you.

For instance, one benchmark many use is how many books an

author publishes in a year. I have a lot of author friends that publish a book every three months. Some publish even more often than that. Would I like to put out novels that quickly and reap the benefits of fast-publishing, keeping new books in front of my readers and constantly having releases? Sure! Of course I would.

But that model is something I simply am not capable of sustaining for so many reasons. For one, I'm a slow processor and that makes me a slower writer. I put out quality content (I hope) but it takes me a little longer because that's just how my brain works. Second, due to time, family and other constraints that are personal to me, I'm not able to give the hours per day to writing that it would take in order for *me* to finish a final draft of a novel every two months. Third, I don't have an assistant. Right now I'm a one-woman show. That means I do it all—writing, marketing, accounting, etc.—which cuts down on the time I can spend on simply writing.

I could continue with the reasons, but the bottom-line is that because of the nature of my methods and choices, my writing experience regarding books published per year looks very different from that of the authors I referenced.

And that's okay.

It's more than okay. It's the way it should be. Comparing my successes, sales, published works, etc., to theirs would be a mistake because, again, I'm not them, I'm me.

Your journey should fit your personality, your life, your dreams, and your preparedness to give to it. Not someone else's. Writing, and especially publishing, has costs to it. Costs of time, money and emotional bandwidth. What you give to your writing and publishing will in some form or fashion be deducted from other areas of your life. So I encourage you to decide not only what your goal is, but what *you* are willing to give to achieve it. What sacrifices are *you* willing to make? Where are *you* going to draw the lines? These answers will largely dictate your writing/publishing experience.

Don't misunderstand me. It's a great idea to identify other authors who seem to be on the same path you want to be on, and learn what they are doing to get the job done. That's just smart. Learn from them and make your plan. But if you find, for whatever reason, that model stops working for you, it's okay to change your approach. To change your goal to something that fits *you* better—whether it's a change in quantity of output, genre, traditional vs. indie, wide vs. exclusive, profit expectations, or something else.

I also don't mean that if it gets hard or overwhelming for a season, you should immediately switch it all up, or worse, quit. Any job can be hard and overwhelming at times. Keep forging ahead. But if you find that the season never ends, that you aren't enjoying writing anymore, and you're doing laundry all the time in order to avoid your writing or publishing responsibilities, it may be time to rethink your approach and/or your goals. That kind of flexibility will help keep you in the "happy, fulfilled" author zone.

If you know what you're willing to give, and you're giving on that level in all aspects of your writing journey, then you are succeeding.

Celebrate *your* accomplishments, *your* milestones. Don't devalue them by measuring them against someone else's.

Though the world might say I'm wrong, I don't believe there is only one definition of success when it comes to writing and publishing. Knowing that truth will set you free as an author.

D.L. Wood, *USA TODAY* bestselling author of suspense and CleanCaptivatingFiction™

Newsletter Signup and Free Short-story
(https://www.subscribepage.com/n3k2k1)
Facebook: https://www.facebook.com/dlwoodonline/
Twitter: https://twitter.com/dlwoodonline
DLWoodOnline.com

S.E. LYNES

RECENTLY, I WAS PART of a panel talk entitled *How to Get Published*. During the Q and A, a representative of the publishing industry advised the audience of aspiring authors keen to pick up useful tips to have faith in themselves. I understood what she meant but, having been an aspiring author myself for many years, I felt the need to contradict her slightly. I told the assembled throng not to worry if they didn't have faith in themselves, that doubt in themselves or a lack of confidence was not necessarily a barrier to success...

We live in a world of internet news both fake and real, of perfect social media bodies and lives, and bumper sticker philosophies blazing in bold fonts from our crowded feeds: Just Be Yourself! Let Your Crazy Shine! What Others Think of You is None of Your Business! We are being bombarded with certainties when what I for one feel most of the time is doubt. And what I wish I'd known back when I was an aspiring author is that doubt, a lack of faith, a lack of confidence, is no barrier to becoming a successful author, so don't worry if you aren't as gung-ho about your work as you'd wish to be.

For me, an author's place is doubt. Doubt is where we live. It's OK, more than OK, to be uncertain, to not know, to lack faith. No author describes their latest work as the answer to a question about a given issue. Authors say things like 'I wanted to explore' or 'I was trying to look at' or 'I was troubled by'. Authors don't profess to have the answers. They offer no definitive truth beyond the myriad contradictory truths of their novel (for more refined thoughts on this, see Milan Kundera's exquisite essay, *The Truth of the Novel*). An author's gift to their reader lies in the infinitesimal shades of grey they present in a given situation, character, opinion, story. They lay out their competing contradictory voices and aim to somehow disentangle them in an attempt to understand them better. In a sense, doubt, or a lack of confidence or certainty or faith or whatever you want to call it, is necessary to becoming a successful author. Y'know…arguably.

If you, an aspiring author, suffer from a lack of confidence in your work and your negotiations with the world, do not lose heart. Novels are not bumper sticker philosophies; they are not neat little epithets by Rumi or Dorothy Parker. The first draft of a novel is a big rickety shed at best in dire need of nails; at worst, to be collapsed and started again. Do you really think that book you just picked up in Waterstones is a first draft of an author who has been writing for six months? Do you actually believe that most authors sit down and write a final, polished piece of art? Do you imagine all those tricksy plot moves, that heart-aching prose, those complicated characters came out fully formed? No. Most books, as any honest author will tell you, involve some planning, yes, some ideas, yes, a bit of story and some sketches of types of people, yes, yes, yes, but also years of practice in handling language not as a day-to-day tool to write emails but as an art form just like any other art form. We do not attempt to learn the oboe and expect to join the orchestra after one year; why should our work be publishable after the same?

A novel requires patience, diligence, accessing and re-accessing the work in different ways, deleting, re-writing, a stroke of luck here, a lick of inspiration there, and always, always doubt: doubt about the validity of the story, about the authenticity of the characters, about whether anyone besides your mum will be interested, whether you are good enough to do justice to the idea, that is if the idea is even worth exploring the first place, doubt about the dialogue, about the unity of the piece as a whole, about whether you, the creator, have leaked into the pages or left your creations to speak and live for themselves…I could go on. Suffice to say, if you have unshakeable faith in your work, you are unlikely to be able to approach it constructively, to hear feedback, to improve.

I know there is a lot of noise, a lot of mental chatter, because I hear it too. But all you can do is keep writing. Accept doubt. Go with it. Keep going. Do your best at the time of writing, try and become comfortable with not being comfortable. This is the only way I have found to keep those voices quiet. Write each day, just crack on – it's the only way to beat the critical id, the doubt, the fears, the jitters, the heebie-jeebies, the lack of faith, whatever you like to call the whispers that say: that's not very good, is it? And all the time you are doing this, you are getting better.

By March 2022 I will be the author of ten published novels. Am I good enough? Yes. And maybe. And probably not. And no. But none of these answers makes any difference. Someone else has had faith in me, and that's what got me published. Me? I work hard, I strive to be better with each book, because it is all I have. Each novel I write is the best I can do *at the time* – if I have faith in anything it is in this and the desire I had to write it. It's possible the book would have been better had I written it a year from now. Or the year before. If I had spent more time on it. Or less. It's also equally possible the novel is the best version of itself simply because, if I wrote it in that moment, it means I was responding to something deep in my psyche which gave rise to the idea – and good stories are always about something other than the mechanics of the fictional narrative.

In short, I don't know if me or my books are good enough. I do my absolute best and send it off but it's not my job to know if it is worthy of publication. I sincerely hope it is, that is all. My job is to keep writing, regardless of whether or not I am published. Because if you think being published removes doubt, either creative or existential, think again. There are cruel critics, anonymous trolls, kinder critics such as your editor, reviews, the terror of public exposure, of being somehow *known,* seen into by strangers or worse, by your friends, your family, to whom you've been pretending to be confident for all these years. It is terribly exposing to be published. I almost didn't go through with it. Even now, the run up to publication day is terribly stressful, the fictional 'what if?' becoming all too real. What if it's a flop? What if everyone hates it? What if everyone hates *me?* The answer to this lack of faith is there is no answer, only action: keep writing, keep going, keep laying out and disentangling those voices. It is all you can do. You are not responsible for anything outside of this task.

One bit of good news is that becoming a published author has, very slowly, made me more confident. The doubt is still there but part of me, somewhere, knows I can do this and my publisher is so supportive that I feel that, even if one day I find myself struggling with an idea, they are there to help me through; they want me to succeed, and that helps more than I can say. Sometimes someone else's faith in you restores your faith in yourself. Becoming a professional author has returned to me a sense of self that I had lost. I am no longer that quaking, shaking thing that almost didn't go through with the publication of my debut, VALENTINA. I still over-think. I still get nervous. I still worry that my editor won't like the next book. But I have learnt to see that side of myself as part of who I am and indeed part of what it means to be a writer. We embrace doubt. We learn to welcome our lack of faith. I certainly need it in order to write psychological suspense, which, for me, exists in the trembling vacuum between the world as it is and the world as I perceive it to be. Scary stuff indeed. If I am still afraid, at least I know where and how I can use that very fear: in my work.

Formerly a BBC producer, S.E. Lynes turned to writing following the birth of her third child. After completing an MA in Creative Writing, she became a tutor at Richmond Adult Community College, where she taught creative writing for over ten years. She now combines writing, mentoring and lecturing.

Susielynes.Wixsite.com/Website

JB LYNN

I CAN'T TELL YOU how many times I rewrote the first few chapters of my first couple of novels.

I'd go over and over them. I'd tweak them based on feedback I'd gotten from friends. I'd rewrite them based on a single detail I'd inserted in a later chapter. I polished them to "perfection" because every piece of advice you read, makes a point of hammering home the idea that you need to make those first couple of chapters "perfect."

I'm not saying they're not important, they absolutely are, but it's more important to finish writing the book because if you don't, you can never submit it. (This applies to fiction writers. Non-fiction book proposals are completely different.)

I can't tell you how many talented writers I've known who have never finished their novel because they've gotten so bogged down in those first few chapters. Admittedly, I am a plotter, so I always know how a book is going to end before I start it, but I used to get mired in the beginning. Just stuck there, flailing around like I was stuck in quicksand, unable to get myself out of the mess I'd stepped into. I'd like to say for days or weeks, but it was often for months.

Or worse, I'd give up altogether. (Yes, I've been guilty of not finishing books. Learn from my mistakes!)

Nothing is ever going to be "perfect." Not your query letter, not your sample pages, and, sorry to say, not even your book. There will always be a moment when it occurs to you that you could have done something different.

My best advice is to finish what you start. Then, and only then, go back and fix it. Take a couple passes and then release it. Channel your inner Elsa and let it go. (I've also known writers who get stuck in the editing phase for years and years.) Move on. If you're querying, start a new book. If you're self-publishing, start a new book. Don't get stuck!

JB Lynn, author of the never-ending Confessions of a Slightly Neurotic Hitwoman series. She also writes the Psychic Consignment Mysteries and the Cursed Chick Club series because she's got a soft spot for hijinks, humor, and heart (not to mention an almost compulsive need to tell stories!).

JBLynn.com

SOUND ADVICE

"Ideas are cheap.... It's the execution that is all important."

— George R.R. Martin

PAT SIMMONS

MILITARY BASES ARE AN author's best friend. And no, you don't need a military connection to be a vendor.

I learned about this gold mine of an opportunity from fellow Christian Vanessa Miller. Back in the day, Vanessa would hit the road and stay at various bases for up to a week. The chick made money and got her name out. Her popularity grew and so did her sales that she earned a spot on Essence's Bestseller's list.

I contacted the closest base to me, which is Scott Air Force Base in Illinois. I developed a relationship with the various store managers at the Exchange. They LOVE vendors because they make a certain percentage profit from our sales. I am still one of the top authors who sign there. If I don't make any sales, I owe them nothing. A deal that you can't pass up, especially when vendor tables cost hundreds of dollars upfront and you pray you to earn it back.

My husband and my road trips took us as far as March Air Force Base in California to Patrick AFB in Florida and others in between.

The benefits:

Leave with cash in your pockets. It wasn't unusual for me to come home with cash in my pocket. Meet servicemen, retirees, and their families from over all the world. If they buy a book and enjoy it, they will tell others back home. They might even purchase books to mail to them.

Increase your subscriber list for your newsletter. I consistently sent out monthly newsletters since 2006, and some of those first fans are still on my list.

Doors open at the bases. Invites to be vendors at federal buildings. One base in Omaha introduced me to a woman whose church invited me in for a woman's tea. This was a paid event.

So, what's the plan:

You can't sit at your table and expect people to come up to you, even readers. You need to stand and greet them before they go into the BX or PX store. Wear comfortable shoes, and a smile, even when people are rude. As a Christian author, I remember one time praying at the base for God to send the people. The Lord Jesus did just that. My husband and I had little cash when we arrived. We made $450 in one day. Praise the Lord. He supplied our needs.

Prepare for a long day. The management only requires authors to stay a couple of hours, but you miss folks. Get there early for those early bird shoppers. Next the mid-day, the mad lunch rush crowd, late afternoon, then the folks who have got off of work. I would have missed these potential buyers only standing a few hours.

No two bases are the same. I've had ones I would never go back to. Wasn't worth my time, travel, and effort. I have repeatedly done well at Nellis AFB, Luke AFB, Ft. Campbell, Little Rock AFB, Ft. Sam Houston, Lackland, Randolph, and Patrick AFB.

Social media is good, but the bases will also open doors for you and put cash in your pocket. The percentage of the Exchange charge varies between 9% to 15%. No sweat. If you don't make money, you owe them nothing. Go for it!

Pat Simmons is a multi-published Christian romance author of more than thirty titles. She is a self-proclaimed genealogy sleuth and a five-time recipient of the RSJ Emma Rodgers Award for Best Inspirational Romance. Pat also holds a B.S. in mass communications from Emerson College in Boston, Massachusetts, and has worked in radio, television, and print media for more than twenty years.

PatSimmons.net

JENIFER RUFF

FEW PEOPLE WILL WRITE a book and instantly become a bestselling author. Those are the lucky ones. For the other ninety-nine-plus percent of us, there's more to it than that. But it's all doable and most of it is enjoyable. Once you get hooked on writing and decide that becoming a "successful author" (of which there are many definitions) is something you seriously want to pursue, treat your writing career like any other career. Expect to commit a significant investment of time and some money to get it going and to maintain it. Trust that your writing business is worth building to the best of your abilities and budget.

Get comfortable with occasionally being very uncomfortable. Some things get easier, but there always seems to be something new ahead. Learning curves are a guaranteed part of your writing, publishing, and marketing journey. Accept and embrace those facts from the start, don't let them deter you. You don't have to master everything.

My current discomfort, for example, comes from TikTok. I'm excited about the opportunities the booktok platform presents, and yet, I would much rather *not* figure it out so I could write, revise, or read a good book with tea and cookies instead. Yet I believe it's worth the trouble to explore if it's going to help me find new readers. To prepare, I'm learning all I can glean from the TikTok author pioneers, taking a course, and spending time on the app. Eventually, I will take a deep breath and dive in with my fingers crossed.

Remember that you aren't alone in this awesome journey. There's a great big, supportive author/publishing community at your fingertips thanks to the internet. Check in often with author groups on social media to learn and get inspired. However, despite all the knowledge sharing available, you will still make mistakes along the way. Some of those mishaps might render you temporarily shellshocked and nauseous, like when I made changes to the back matter of dozens of manuscripts in the wee hours of the morning, uploaded the wrong file for one digital book, and it went out to thousands of readers in a big promo a few days later. You will get through those challenges and have great stories to share with those beginning their writing endeavors after you.

Don't worry about trying to be everything to everyone with your stories. People have different tastes. What appeals to some does not appeal to all. But do pick a genre and stick with it. Aim for a slow and steady accumulation of readers and sales to manage your expectations and don't give up. Keep writing. Keep editing. Keep marketing. Keep learning. Repeat. Eventually, probably sooner than later, the rewards and the sense of accomplishment will make it worth all your efforts.

Jenifer Ruff is a *USA Today* bestselling author who writes twisty mystery thrillers, including the award-winning Agent Victoria Heslin series.

JeniferRuff.com

STACY GREEN

THERE ARE A HUNDRED things I wish I'd known when I first started writing, but the one that stands out is remembering that everyone's journey is different. Getting your butt in the chair and writing has a lot of merit, but it's crucial to understand your own goals and capabilities instead of following someone else's script.

I spent years kicking myself because I couldn't write 5000-10,000 words a day like so many indie authors were able to do, and I couldn't just decide to forgo sleep and write because no matter what I did, my brain didn't work that way. Since I started writing in 2012, I couldn't find a way to dig deep enough to be as disciplined as some other writers, which made writing even more of a struggle because I was constantly comparing. I was finally diagnosed with ADHD this year, and everything changed. I am learning to find my routine, my strengths, and realizing that I'm not lazy or unmotivated. I'm wired differently.

You may not have ADHD, but it's okay to struggle to get started and hate rough drafts. Every writer has their own issues, and it's never as easy as it might appear from the outside looking in. I would have told my younger self to shut out all the noise and focus on your skills and how to be productive. Incorporating writing into your daily routine is vital, but you can't be militant if that doesn't work for you. I would have asked my younger self to pay attention to my natural rhythms instead of trying to do the same thing someone else was doing when deep down, I knew it wouldn't work for me.

Now, I can spend six hours in my office a day and I am 100% more productive than just a couple of years ago. I've learned that having a production plan is crucial, even if you're able to make changes. The calendar is your friend, word count trackers are vital, but just because yours are lower than someone else's doesn't mean you're doing it wrong. Understanding your strengths and weaknesses helps you anticipate ups and downs in your schedule, and even if you aren't a planner, it's important to have some sort of road map.

The other component is practice make perfect. As basic as it sounds, the more you write, the better you get. The more you read, the better you understand story structure, even if you don't like plotting ahead. Understanding the impact of structure and the key points within it are vital to a good story. There are plenty of good craft books, but reading books in my genre and studying what made them work helped me understand structure and craft better than anything else.

Writers like to say they do it because they love writing and telling stories, and that's true. But every single one of us experiences self-doubt and flat-out loathing for our WIP at least once, and it happens to most of us with every book. Writing isn't always fun, even if you don't consider it a business or your primary job. But for me, it's getting over those humps, figuring out the plot issues and putting the pieces together correctly that makes every book its own amazing experience.

Stacy Green, *USA Today* best-selling author of more

than a dozen mysteries and thrillers. Her books include the award-winning Lucy Kendall series, the Cage Foster series, and the *USA Today* best-selling Nikki Hunt series.

StacyGreenAuthor.com

GRIFF HOSKER

WHEN I WAS ASKED to write this piece it made me reflect on my journey from teacher to writer. The truth is I always wanted to write. Growing up in 1950s England we had a lesson called composition and it was my favourite. A fertile imagination helped me. Of course, I knew I could not simply start writing stories at 15 and become successful and so I became a teacher but the dream of being a writer was still there. The English/Drama degree I studied actually honed my skills but I did not know it. We wrote and performed plays for our fellow students. Once I embarked on a 40-year career in inner-city schools I continued to try to become a writer but I am afraid that the cabal of publishers is very much a closed shop. With the help of typewriters bought for me as Christmas presents by my mother I sent manuscript after manuscript to publishers, the BBC, in fact, anyone I could. 90% of what I sent was returned unopened and was very depressing. Luckily I had an audience to write for in my schools and that constant demand for material helped me to learn to type quickly.

It was only when I retired in 2010 that I applied myself to the process of becoming a writer and it was the Arts Council programme, Feedaread that allowed me to do so. I self-published in paperback with them. I sold about five books and that was to friends but I had been published and believe it or not that lit a fire under me and I wrote another four books quickly. It was

Amazon kindle that was my saviour. E-books were the way ahead and I soon found that there was an audience out there. However, I should insert a caveat. I was not diligent enough about my editing and tried to do it alone. Every writer needs an editor. I was lucky in that my wife was able to do that. The second lesson I learned, a year or so into the process was that the old adage is right and a good cover sells the book. My son, who now runs the business side of the company found an excellent design company and my sales leapt from 6,000 copies a month to 12,000 a month in six months! Well worth the investment.

Thanks to a life of work that began when I was fifteen and early mornings being part of that I find that a routine is vital to a writer. I start work at 6- reading and replying to readers' emails. Then I read through the previous day's writing, editing and correcting before beginning work on my 5000-word target. I am a little obsessive about that but I find it helps and keeps up with the demands of my readers who want a new book every month.

How do I come up with storylines? Easy. I look to history and find those nuggets that are often overlooked. I trawl through my memory of people and places so that my books are populated by real people. I listen to how people speak, and their mannerisms. I watch them in their natural habitats. They say if you have ever met a writer then you will be in a novel and that is true.

I am often asked about research and I find that the easiest part of the job. Thanks to the internet and my extensive library I can find almost everything I want in my little sanctuary of an office. I also try to write about the land close to my home. As there are twenty odd castles and Hadrian's Wall all within an hour or so of driving I can get boots on the ground any time I like. My readers also help me and they are the first to correct any omission, no matter how minor. I cannot stress highly enough the value of such input.

I have left to the end the thorny subject of traditional publishing. As I said at the beginning self-publishing has made me what I am but a few years ago I was headhunted by a company to write a series of books for them. Vanity got the better of me and I agreed. In hindsight that was a mistake. Firstly because they gave me a tenth of what I was earning through self-publication and the slight increase in sales did not offset the loss. Secondly, they control everything and I like being in control of costs, prices, titles, length of novel and so forth. Needless to say when the contract ended so did my association. It seems to me that new writers will be overlooked by publishers who want proven names or someone an agent recommends. I have no agent. To me, they are a boys' club, a closed shop. Self-publication is a way of life and I have embraced it.

If any aspiring writer wishes advice then just get in touch with me. I have helped more than half a dozen writers to get published. One is on her fourth book and another on his fifth. I know what it is like to feel alone and without any help. I promise I will reply to any email you send to me and my advice will be honest.

Good luck.

Griff Hosker - Home of Epic Fiction

www.griffhosker.com

LISA MORTON

WHAT DO I WISH Younger Me had known? This:

It's okay to be confident, especially if you identify as female.

Why would anyone need to hear this? Here's the thing that a lot of my male writer friends don't understand: when you grow up as a girl in this culture, you get a lot of conditioning that tells you to pull back, to (at least pretend to) be demure, to let men take the lead. That conditioning can come in all kinds of forms, everything from television commercials to parental advice. Consequently, by the time a girl becomes a woman she may find herself having to fight her own impulses to fade into the background.

It's okay to tell that part of yourself, "No." But don't just say, "No, I'm not going to hold back." Rather, say, "I'm talented and hard-working and I'm not afraid to stand shoulder-by-shoulder with my peers." This is not to say you need to be arrogant, or, even worse, disrespectful and cruel to others. It means you respect yourself along with your fellow authors.

Writing, even more than most other pursuits, is extremely competitive. Whether you choose to go the traditional or indie route (or hybrid), you'll be up against hundreds, *thousands*, of other writers, all vying to get their works in front of readers' eyes. This is where you cannot afford to let others walk in front of you. Don't be afraid to submit your work. Don't be afraid to risk criticism and rejection. Don't be afraid to talk to other writers, even those who you might think are out of your reach (hint: they probably aren't). Don't be afraid of internet trolls who may bully you on social media. Stand above them. *Your work has value.*

If you're wondering how much of this I may have experienced... well, all of it. I had to learn at some point to stand proud, to walk right up to editors and ask if they'd read my work, to not be dismissive of my own skills, to walk that fine line between modesty and strength.

This is why, for years now, I've given a single two-word piece of advice to women authors (or any other author who may have had their self-assurance stripped out): *Be bold.* You can apply that mantra to both your work (don't be afraid to write about *anything*), and to yourself. Embrace confidence. You might be surprised at the results. I know I was.

Lisa Morton, screenwriter, author of non-fiction books, and prose writer whose work has been described by the American Library Association's Readers' Advisory Guide to Horror as "consistently dark, unsettling, and frightening."

LisaMorton.com

MIRANDA RIJKS

'AVOIR DU COURAGE!' MY GP told me. (French is his first language.) I promptly burst into tears because after eleven rounds of the harshest chemotherapy for bone cancer and an operation to remove and replace my femur, I thought I had been extremely courageous. It turns out he wasn't talking about what I'd been through, but the next stage in my life. For all cancer survivors there's the proverbial line in the sand - the before and after. One thing that a life-shock brings is the deep desire for reappraisal. I didn't want to be the person I was before; the person who was too afraid of failure to really try to achieve my greatest dream: to be a full-time author.

I've always written. As a child I would compose lengthy stories. When my daughter was young, I made up a different story using the same characters every single night. As a mature adult, I studied the craft and completed a Masters in Writing. I was the author of a self-help book (published by Bloomsbury, no less) and a biography, yet I never dared call myself an author. For some bizarre reason I felt that until I was a published writer of fiction, I didn't have the right to define myself as an author.

Having been given a second chance at life, I realised that the only thing that had stopped me from releasing my fiction into the world was fear. Fear that my writing wasn't good enough. Fear that constant rejection would eat away my fragile sense of self-worth.

But now, having stared death in the face on several occasions, fear of rejection seemed rather trivial. Besides, the publishing landscape had changed, and I no longer needed the endorsement of an agent and a publishing house. I could go it alone.

I had an overwhelming urge to write a novel about a protagonist who had cancer and survived, happier and stronger than before. So many novels about cancer have sad endings yet these days more people survive than die. I paid over the odds for an editor and cover designer but that didn't matter because writing *Don't Call Me Brave* was so cathartic. I studied the self-publishing market and decided I wouldn't even try to get a publisher for my future books. But so often things don't go the way we plan. I released my first psychological thriller (*I Want You Gone*) in November 2018 and at the beginning of January 2019, I received an email from my current publishers asking to talk to me. I was hugely cynical because who other than vanity publishers approach an author? My experience of mainstream publishers had been lacklustre at best. Small advances, pathetic royalties, having to do the marketing myself, etc. But these guys were most definitely not vanity publishers, and they had a knowledgeable answer to all my questions. At that point I had little to lose. As I write this article, I am working on psychological thriller number fourteen and have been an Amazon bestseller several times over. As a writer, you need to be flexible and grab every opportunity that comes your way.

Looking back, I realise that writing is my therapy. Writing psychological thrillers allows me to explore my greatest fears in the safe confines of a book. It allows me to step out of my everyday world and get much needed perspective. I don't tend to have regrets, but

I wish I'd come to that conclusion years ago. I might have focused more on the enjoyment of the process and less on the outcome. This article has given me the chance to ask, should I have started writing fiction at a younger age? (My first psychological thriller was published when I was 52!) Surprisingly, the answer is no. Whilst there are many brilliant young writers, personally I've been able to bring my wide-ranging life experiences to my writing and I hope it gives my thrillers an authenticity that I wouldn't have been able to tap into earlier in life.

Nevertheless, it would have been helpful to explain to my younger self what some of the foundation stones are for writing success. Here is my list:

1. Be good at your craft. My problems lay with over-writing, unbelievable characters and muddling up time lines. I've worked hard on those points. It's not necessary to do a degree in writing but it is essential to get honest feedback from an objective editor. Friends and family don't count.

2. Have a writing buddy or hire a book coach. Writing can be lonely. My publishers work with their authors to map out detailed plots before we start writing. If you're a plotter like me, then hire a book coach or find someone to bounce plot ideas off. If you're a 'pantster' and prefer to write without a plot, be prepared for considerable editing.

3. Don't think that your first book will be great. I have several completed manuscripts that will never see the

light of day. You need to put in your ten thousand plus hours to become an expert in your craft.

4. Write because you love the process. Write because you have stories that you want to tell. The process matters way more than the outcome. If you don't enjoy the process, then find something else that you love doing.

5. It's an exciting time to be an author as there are many different ways to get your book in front of readers. If you're self-publishing, view it like a business. You need to invest both time and money. Have a plan and prepare to run at a loss. If you've been offered a publishing contract, get it checked over by an official body such as The Society of Authors (in the UK). You can and should negotiate. You don't need an agent or a mainstream publisher, digital-first publishers can bring you great success.

6. If you're seeking commercial fiction success, that's fine, but be aware of the pitfalls. Study your genre very carefully and make sure you keep to the tropes. Romance readers expect a happy ending. Psychological thriller readers want to be kept guessing. The same goes for your book cover. Make sure it looks like other covers in your genre. Boring, you might think, and yes, you're right. But newbie authors in particular, can't break the mould.

7. Develop a thick skin. Don't read every review.

Celebrate when you get your first one-star review. Realise that if someone writes a particularly horrible review it speaks more about them than it does about your book (particularly if you've got plenty of four- or five-star reviews). You're never going to please everyone.

8. It's very rare that financial success comes from one book. If you want to make a living from being an author, be prepared to write multiple books.

9. Luck. Everyone needs a big dollop of luck.

Miranda Rijks is the bestselling author of fourteen gripping psychological thrillers including *The Visitors*, *The Arrangement* and *The New Neighbour*. Her twisty novels are set in England, where she lives. When she's not writing, she's dreaming about living in a chalet on a Swiss mountain, obsessively knitting, painting on her iPad or coming up with crazy business ideas.

MirandaRijks.com

RHONDA MCKNIGHT

I WISH I'D KNOWN my writing would be bigger than me.

I worked in a bookstore and at my local library as a teenager. I loved fiction. I'd been writing since I was six years old. I'd dreamed of being a novelist as a pre-teen. Because of my love for books, I enjoyed both jobs immensely, but in some respects, they affected me negatively. There were so few fiction books on the shelves by Black authors that I never imagined I could be an author. I didn't see myself, therefore I didn't believe there was a place for me, so I put my pen down and pushed that dream out of my head.

I revisited my dream in the late 90's because Terry McMillian, Beverly Jenkins, and Victoria Christopher Murray were on bestseller list. Sharon Ewell Foster won the Christy Award. Black writers were making some strides. I decided it wasn't too late to write my book.

My first novel was released by a traditional publisher in 2009. There was no better feeling than walking into Walmart and the bookstore and the library and seeing my book on the shelf. Since then, I have written twenty-five traditional and indie published novels. Over the years, there have been times when I've been overwhelmed by the accolades and gratitude aspiring Black authors extend to me. They see me on the shelf and believe they can sit alongside me.

When people say representation matters, it *really* does. It's not just a trendy phrase or a hashtag or even an excuse. For marginalized and under-represented groups, representation *is* aspirational evidence that there is a path to their dream. So, I would tell my younger self, write, and push for a publishing deal. Write for every Black woman before you who could only dream of writing because there was no where she could push. There weren't few opportunities, there were no opportunities. The doors to publishing houses weren't just closed to her. They were locked.

I am my ancestors' wildest dream. I am someone's inspiration and a mentor to many. If I had known when I was getting started that my writing career was all bigger than me, I would have started sooner.

Rhonda McKnight is the author of several award-winning novels and Black Expressions Top 20 bestsellers, including An *Inconvenient Friend, What Kind of Fool* and *Breaking All The Rules*. She is the winner of the 2015 *Emma* Award for Inspirational Romance of the Year. She was also a 2010 nominee for the African-American Literary Award. Rhonda writes edgy stories that touch the heart of women. The themes of faith, forgiveness and hope mark her stories.

RhondaMcknight.com

CHRIS FABRY

I REMEMBER WALKING PAST a bookstore at the corner of Chicago Avenue and LaSalle Street in downtown Chicago. This was around 1987. I stopped and stared into that store, scanned the shelves, and vowed one day I would see a book with my name on it.

If I could go back and stand beside myself as I looked in that window, knowing the longing to express the words and stories that bubbled inside, here's what I would say.

You think your goal is to be published. You think success is having a book on a shelf with your name on it. That's not a bad goal. Publication is a good step. But there's something bigger going on here.

After you've had a few books with your name on it on those shelves, you're going to think success is a big paycheck. Royalties. Again, it's not a bad goal to be able to feed your family. But success in the writing life can't be measured by your bank account.

I see your eyes glazing over. It's probably because publication seems so far away. You don't even know if you can call yourself a writer. Trust me. If you spend time with your rear in the chair putting words on the page, trying to muster the faith to believe you have something to say, you're a writer.

Are you listening? This is important.

Focus on the process, not the goal. The most important thing to come from your writing is not a paycheck or an ego boost. It's not even changing the world one reader at a time. Not a bad thing to happen as a result, but you don't control the results. All you can do is tell the best story you can, write one true sentence after another like Papa said, and allow the process to do its work in here. (Taps his chest.)

On your wall, a few years from now, you'll have a quote from Old Man Hemingway. "Write hard and clear about what hurts." Do that with all your heart. Every day. Don't give up. Mine your life like your grandfather dug for coal. Let your heart be broken and poured out on every page. Make yourself laugh with your writing. Cry. Your success is not measured by the externals but the internals. What is going on inside of you in these next few years is more important than awards and sales numbers.

Don't give up.

Write your heart out.

Believe you are a writer in spite of what the inner voices say.

And don't give up.

Chris Fabry is an award-winning author and radio personality who hosts the daily program Chris Fabry Live on Moody Radio.

ChrisFabry.com

SHERRI WINSTON

STORYTELLING. I'VE BEEN MAKING up stories since I was two. My mom and dad used to enjoy telling a story about me, when I'd come home from an outing with my dad and told my mom he'd taken me to visit his other wife and family. Now, I was told that I went on to describe multiple "brothers and sisters" that my dad had secretly with my other "mom."

As you can imagine, this did not go over well with dear ol' mom until the two deciphered that my avid imagination was alive and well.

It's a good story, but it's not a book. It's not the secret to being an author.

What I wish I'd known earlier in my life is the difference between a good story and a well-written novel. Stories get told at dinner parties; books get written after thoughtful construction, smoothed out with ample imagination, then sculpted with more thought and lots of editing.

Even though I spent most of my professional life as a journalist, I didn't truly learn or distinguish between a creatively written piece and a creative idea until I spent a year as a University of Michigan Fellow in Journalism, where I studied creative writing.

Through the rigor of the program, and with the thoughtful consideration of a few professors, I managed to write a piece that got me into a writer's group. From there, I used that same writing to impress the group leader, who ultimately introduced me to her agent, who then shepherded the project from novella to finished novel to published. Here's what I learned:

- Know the difference between an idea and a story.

- Respect the process.

- Understand that the idea is just the beginning; that's the part you tell friends when you say, "Hey, you guys, I've got this idea."

- What follows is the work. Haunt writer's groups or writing magazines. Read what others have tried in the name of taking an idea to the next phase.

- Find a good mentor who can pull you back from the abyss—which is when you are spending more time "learning" about writing than actually writing.

- Don't be afraid to write poorly. It's a first draft. Write as much of it as you have in your head or soul. Edit later, once you've had a chance to really sit and look at the idea.

- Be fearless. It's scary out here in these author streets. We have to set aside our fears of being humiliated by our "bad" writing. Instead, use that energy to elevate what you have.

- Also, don't fear innovation. If your plot is built on the altar of lookalike plots, that's not always a bad thing. However, to stand out, maybe your boy + girl could have a boy who lives beneath the sea with his family on their oceanic observation lab while the girl is the mermaid his family is determined to prove doesn't exist. Just a thought.

I hope my story helps. My very best wishes to all. I know it can feel like a Sisyphean task. However, keep pushing, and one day you will get that rock up the hill. Promise!

Sherri Winston is the author of *President of the Whole Fifth Grade*, as well as her latest book, *Lotus Bloom and the Afro Revolution*, which was long listed for a National Book Award.

VoteForCupcakes.com
SherriWinston.com

LISA HARRIS

I WANTED TO BE a writer for as long as I can remember. I have chapters of handwritten stories stashed away in a worn box that I started writing while I was in junior high. That love of writing came, I'm sure, from a love of reading. Throughout my childhood, I spent every free moment engrossed in books, and those stories spurred my own imagination and made me dream of becoming a published author one day. Because I loved mysteries and Nancy Drew, I started with my own version of a teen-girl detective story. Later I read the Diary of Anne Frank, and wrote a story about a girl caught up in the horrors of the holocaust. The first book I actually finished was a gothic novel inspired by Victoria Holt who had this amazing gift of bringing characters and intriguing settings to life. Each book I read imprinted on me the love of story, adventure, romance, tragedy, and redemption. Powerful stories that managed to tug on my heartstrings and kept me turning the page to the very end. But writing my own stories has been its own journey of challenges, joy, and discovery.

Here are three things I wish I'd known about writing.

    1. It's a marathon and not a sprint.

When I started writing, I remember reading the first chapter of my novel out loud to my critique group. I was unpublished, but convinced that I had a gripping best-seller on my hands. At least that's what I thought until they told me the truth. They recommended that I take my chapter home and rewrite it because my wonderful characters were nothing more than cardboard figures.

Ouch.

It hurt, and yet hearing the truth is what pushed me forward. I discovered that night that writing is a journey, and forty plus books later, I'm still learning, taking classes, and reading. The process has been both exhilarating and challenging. I love the anticipation of discovering what happens next in a story, of fleshing out characters, and that moment when it all comes together. The process of taking ideas, building on them, and weaving them together is magical. Some of the characters come unannounced, begging to have their story written down. Others I have to struggle to get to know. The process of bringing their stories to life, though, always involves layering plotlines, drawing from the setting, developing characters, then editing, brainstorming, lots of scribbled notes, reworking timelines, and more editing. In the end, if I've done my job, I can share a story that does exactly what I love about a good book. . .Tugs on readers' heartstrings and keeps them turning the pages.

2. You don't have to do it all.

I always imagined myself sitting in some cabin somewhere, churning out bestsellers. And yet most authors quickly discover that in today's world, there is more to 'writing' then simply sitting down and penning a story. It doesn't take long to get sucked into all the things you *must* do in order to shove your story to the top of the algorithms and get noticed. You've got to post regularly on Pinterest, Instagram, TikTok, and Facebook, leave comments in all your groups, write monthly newsletters—

Stop.

Let me just repeat number two. You don't have to do it all. Find what works for you as far as promotion, but never forget your love for words and story in the process. Give yourself permission to step away and focus on your story.

3. Enjoy the journey.

If I didn't love writing, I don't think I would still be creating stories two decades later. And yet, I really do love the process. The inkling of a story line that begins to come to life, the characters emerge, plot twists threaten to send my heroes over the edge. . .Writing for me continues to be an adventure I don't think I'll ever tire of. And beyond the writing, there's the life-time friends I've made on this journey of both writers and readers. So if you want to be in this for the long haul, remember to slow down and stop along the way, don't think you have to do everything, and enjoy the journey.

Lisa Harris is a *USA Today* bestselling author, a Christy Award finalist for *Blood Ransom*, *Vendetta* and *Port of Origin*, Christy Award winner for *Dangerous Passage*, and the winner of the Best Inspirational Suspense Novel for 2011 (*Blood Covenant*) and 2015 (*Vendetta*) from Romantic Times. She has forty plus novels and novellas in print.

LisaHarrisWrites.com

J.J. MILLER

OKAY, THE FIRST THING I wish I'd had instilled in me years ago is this: don't think yourself into a corner. Divorce yourself from the idea that there's just the one and only book for you to write.

I tried writing a novel in my thirties only to lose my way. I was fixated on it but had no idea where to take the story. This effort was not out of the blue—I'd written many magazine articles by then—but I never made it far beyond half a dozen chapters. I lost all confidence. Jettisoned with this project was the notion that I could, would, or should ever write a novel.

Then in my fifties, I wrote—as in completed—my first novel. Totally different story from my first attempt, and one that my younger self could never have envisioned. I self-published this book and watched for weeks as practically no one bought it. Then, amazingly, it climbed into Amazon's top-paid 200.

This surprised the hell out of me. I'd been convinced for so long that fiction was not my bag.

So, don't pin everything on that first novel, the one you feel that you need to get out. The one you are fixated on. The one you are hanging every hope of being an author on. The one you can't finish writing. Its whole point might be nothing more than a support act for something better, later.

The next thing I wish I'd taken to heart is that there's no set path to being a successful author.

While I loved to read novels, I didn't always have my head buried in one. And I didn't have the discipline to be always scribbling down notes as a "true writer" was supposed to do.

What I did have was a kind of friendship with writing. I found that I had a good turn of phrase. This was different from my real-world interactions with people. I struggled with small talk. I sucked at telling jokes. I never felt I was a natural storyteller.

Maybe these verbal deficiencies steered me towards writing, maybe not. But in writing, I discovered a voice that felt authentic, something that reflected a truer, fuller me.

I found this out in the first years of high school when, on the rare occasion, we were given a creative writing assignment. When my stories were read to the class, I got the first sense of having pleased an audience. What a humbling thrill that was.

When I went traveling, I got to practice that turn-of-phrase thing I so enjoyed. I loved composing long letters to my mother and friends back home. And this was not a divine talent.

A good turn of phrase is essentially the act of making language a plaything; coming up with a fresh way to say something. For me, that was often the result of trying to be either funny or honest. In the unsolicited feedback I got from people, it was wonderful to know that something I'd written had resonated with them. This pure, real human connection is writing's core value, isn't it?

Buoyed by this experience, I kept at it. And that's ultimately what I built my writing career on—the recreational pleasure I found in crafting a good line. And that brings me to the rule that underscores everything about writing as I know it, and as such it's the most useful thing I ever learned.

A magazine editor once taught me to "never assume you have a captive audience."

Apply this to every paragraph of every chapter of everything you write for public consumption and you will serve your reader well, I think. And that's the goal—serving the reader. Not your ego.

No one but your mother has to read your first line, your first page, your first chapter. They have better things to do, better things to read. If you don't consider yourself to be the host of a real live person whose attention you value then go do something else. The worst writer to read is convinced that they're interesting or clever, or who is aloof, or is a literary show-off, or who just rambles on and takes me for granted, my patience thinning with every word.

Don't be that writer.

Another vital thing I wished I'd known is the virtue of boundaries. Whenever I heard novelists talk about pages or characters writing themselves, it was like they had access to some marvelous voodoo that I'd never know. I was convinced there was God-given magic to their imagination that I was not blessed with.

In the same vein, I once believed that creative writing was an artistic gift that couldn't be summoned by something so crass and external as a deadline. But this is the biggest load of BS in the writing world.

To write a novel, I need boundaries.

Structure. Plot. Planning. Total word count. These things set a story's boundaries. They form the sandbox of your story. They help ensure you don't stray off course or make a wrong turn or waste your time writing pages that don't deserve to be read. They help prevent you from being self-indulgent.

Boundaries are not creativity's handcuffs. Quite the opposite. They are more like the imagination's glasshouse.

Leonardo Da Vinci produced the Mona Lisa in a space no bigger than a doormat. Consider what it would be like to watch Roger Federer play tennis in the absence of the game's regulations and points system. His athletic artistry flourishes inside a purpose-built box of rules, lines, and conditions. If not for them, we'd just be watching him hit a ball over a net.

And this is something I wish I'd known: that I can and should write on command. Believe me, I can procrastinate with the best of them. I can sit around all day wondering this or that or wait for a phrase or a theme or something that will make a story gel in my head.

Sitting and thinking can only get you so far. Nothing, I repeat nothing, beats the act of writing itself. Think about the scene you're going to write about and what's going to happen. Put a timer on for ten minutes. Hit start and go. Just write. Whatever you end up with is better than a blank page. You now have some clay to rework, refine and polish. Build that time up to forty minutes and you'll have about 1,500 words of clay. And it's highly likely that in that clay will be something good that you could never have thought of just by sitting there. This is the "magic" of discovery that the very act of writing can wield.

The last thing I'd say is that I'd never tell an aspiring writer to "write what you know." This tends to make young writers with limited life experience lean too heavily on autobiography. At least, this was the prohibitive effect such "wisdom" had on me.

You don't have to be a cop to write a crime novel. You don't have to be a time-traveling paranormal shape-shifting lighthouse keeper's daughter to write, you know, that kind of novel. Better advice might be to write what you love to read. But don't even be constrained by that.

Write what you want to explore. Have fun looking into that field and learning about it until you think you can sound authentic.

Writers are actors, in a sense. The author's voice is a role we play, a costume we put on.

It's your sandbox. You can build whatever you like.

If you possess that consistent urge to jump into that sandbox and toy with words, I'd encourage you to indulge in both the work and the play of it. You might just build something quite a few people like.

At that point, you may never want to jump out.

J.J. Miller, Amazon bestselling author of the *Brad Madison* and *Cadence Elliott* legal thriller series. J.J.'s books are filled with intrigue, vivid characters, riveting courtroom drama, and twists you won't see coming.

JJMillerBooks.com

JOANNA CAMPBELL SLAN

THINKING BACK OVER MY career, I can't count the number of times somebody told me I wouldn't or couldn't succeed. They weren't trying to be mean. They were trying to be realistic. And they were wrong. They only saw one path for me. I'm too hard-headed and too creative to be confined to one narrow walkway.

Here's the truth I live—and you are welcome to borrow it and use it as your own—

The only person who can limit your success is you. When you give up, when you quit, when you walk away, then you choose the path to failure.

When you keep going, when you solicit information and use it to improve, and when you never give up, you choose the path to success.

Notice there's a cost to traveling the path to success. You have to 1.) keep going 2.) solicit more information 3.) use it and 4.) keep trying.

For example, my initial publisher dropped the Kiki Lowenstein Mystery Series. The marketing department decided they wanted to take the imprint a different way, and my books didn't fit their new model. I was free to write more books in the series, but they would continue to own and sell books one through six.

Of course, I was crushed. I gave myself time to have a pity party. Then I pulled up my big girl panties and tried to find a way forward.

I was told by other, more experienced authors that if I expanded the series, those early books would continue to sell and make money *for the publisher.* As long as those books were profitable for the publisher, I would never get the rights back.

I approached the publisher and learned that, indeed, they planned to keep selling books one through six. They were happily making money from the series.

Meanwhile, other authors also found themselves dropped by that publisher. Several of those authors retaliated by bad-mouthing the publisher. I never did. In fact, I wrote everyone I'd worked with a letter, thanking them for helping me start my career. After all, those people gave me a chance. Why shouldn't I remain grateful?

It's true that I wasn't happy about their final business decision, but as my husband always reminds me, "It's just business. It's not personal." Despite being dropped, I maintained a cordial relationship with my old publisher.

I decided to continue the series and publish it independently. I started the narrative at book seven and went on. Yes, there was a possibility I'd share revenue with the old publisher, but sharing something was better than having nothing. As long as I kept writing, my new books would find new readers. After a while, I decided to write a book that would serve as an introduction to the extended series, just in case readers started with book seven and not at the beginning. That worked rather well.

Every year, I politely contacted the initial publisher and asked if I could get the rights back. I offered to pay for all the paper books (one through six) they still had in their warehouse. After many years of saying no, finally, they said yes. It took us several months to come to terms. I bought all the inventory in their warehouse. They gave me the printers' files but not the covers. I had new covers made, and I republished the books, aligning them with what I'd written during that period of separation.

What did I learn?

1. Be gracious even if you are dropped.

2. Thank everyone. Publishing is a small business. A lot of the people I worked with are now involved in other publishing ventures.

3. Have faith in your product. I believed in Kiki and the legion of fans who loved her.

4. Be willing to put your money into your business. Invest in yourself.

5. Don't take no as an answer. Politely keep asking!

6. Remember: The publisher doesn't own your fans. You do, especially if you have a great email list.

7. Write your next book. It's the best marketing tool you'll ever have.

Since then, I've been an Amazon bestseller countless times. I've made much, much more money by being independently published than I ever did through traditional publishing. In fact, we've sold close to a half a million copies of my Kiki books since my original publisher and I parted ways. Later this year I'll be publishing *Mask, Or, Raid: Book #18 in the Kiki Lowenstein Mystery Series,* and my fans will be happy for the chance to spend more time with a character they love.

The people who told me it couldn't be done meant well. They were speaking from their experience. They were trying to be helpful. But they were wrong.

Now it's my turn to give advice. Here it is: You can do anything. Anything! Just keep your cool and carry on. You might not succeed right away, but you'll definitely fail if you choose to give up.

New York Times and USA Today bestselling author Joanna Campbell Slan is the author of more than 70 books. She's written both fiction and non-fiction. Learn more at http://www.JoannaSlan.com. Contact her for information about presenting programs for writers at jcslan@joannaslan.com

CHEYENNE MCCRAY

I HAD PLANNED ON being an author since kindergarten, when I read wonderous stories that swept me away, even at that young age, and I wanted to do what those authors did. Years passed and I ended up in careers far from being an author, and for a while I lost the dream. I came to think I wasn't good enough. A pivoting point came as my mom and I were cleaning the kitchen at our family ranch and my mom asked me about my dream. I told her I didn't think I could do it and I didn't think I would ever do it. She actually got mad at me because I had lost something I had dreamed about since I was five years old. It made me think, and I remembered how important that dream had been to me, and that I needed to chase it.

If I had known how my career would take off, and that I would make my living being an author within a span of two years' time, I would have worked toward it long before I did. I would have gathered the courage and made it happen. I am grateful for my twenty plus years as a published author, and grateful that my dream came alive and took wings.

What I would say to those who dream of being an author is to go for it. Fight for it. Never let go of that dream. You'll have ups and downs but do everything you can to learn the craft and work with like-minded writers who are as hungry as you are, then find authors who have advanced in their career and learn from them.

Read books and articles on writing, read novels in the genre you write in, get involved in critique groups, join organizations in your chosen genre, attend conferences, and soak it all in. While you do all of that, keep putting pen to paper and never give up on your dream.

Cheyenne McCray, award-winning New York Times and USA Today bestselling fiction author with over 100 titles and millions of books sold worldwide. Cheyenne also writes cozy mysteries as Deb Ries.

DebRiesBooks.com
CheyenneMcCray.com

G. G. VANDAGRIFF

WHEN I WAS NINE years old, I wrote my first book. It didn't really have a title or a plot. It was a series of adventures by my alter ego—a little girl with golden ringlets named Sandy O'Hara. She had a Scottie dog and best friends who were twins. It was heavily illustrated with drawings in my favorite colors: raw umber, magenta, and aquamarine. I spent many happy times writing these adventures. My Aunt Bette encouraged me, prophesying that I would be an "authoress."

Writing was how I played. I had a twin love—reading. I read everything I could get my hands on. My friends and I had slumber parties where we made up stories. One of us would start, and then the other would pick up the thread. We stayed up late in the night fashioning our future lives in the form of these adventures and love stories.

In high school, I left Sandy behind. But I read more and more. My writing was all academic. The great goal in my life was to get admitted to Stanford University. At the time, it was even a greater challenge than it is today, for the admission policy was to take two-thirds male students and only one-third female. When I was admitted, I was over the moon.

However, this almost became the death knell for my writing. My freshman English teacher called me into his office and said, "Gail, you have a talent for writing. However, in order to progress further, you are going to have to give up your religion."

I believed him. So, when he recommended me for a creative writing seminar, I was daunted. I dried up. It turned out that if I couldn't write about good and evil, I couldn't write. My writing voice refused to produce, and I dropped out of the seminar.

But the urge to express myself in fiction still lived inside me. When I was twenty-seven, I began writing a saga—my own version of War and Peace. It was about the dissolution of the Austrian Empire. It never occurred to me that it might be too weighty a task. I was writing it for myself because I absolutely had to write. I very stubbornly wrote it in my own voice (with perhaps a touch of Tolstoy). I wrote it before and after I had my babies, I wrote while they grew up. I was still writing when they went to college. I didn't have enough confidence in my voice, but I knew my plot was solid.

Then the heavens smiled upon me, and Natalie Goldberg touched my life with her iconic *Writing Down the Bones*. A dear friend, Vicki Flake, and I formed our own writing group, doing Goldberg's writing exercises and then reading the results to one another. This was a life-changer. My friend was very talented. No one had ever told her what to write and what not to write, and she had supreme confidence in her own voice. Goldberg unlocked it, and my friend wrote with joy. About anything. She could make cleaning house sound life-altering.

My secret bugga-boo (my freshman English teacher) was finally gagged and thrown in the corner. For the composition stage of my writing, I put my editor's voice in the closet and let my creative voice roam freely. I grew my self-confidence.

One day my writing exercise produced the first page of a mystery novel. I went on to write it. And quite quickly, I went on to publish it. My confidence in my writing grew, and I produced a series. I continued to write light fiction, but *The Last Waltz* was always in the back of my head. I rewrote it, finally.

When I appeared in my editor's office with a 500-page manuscript, she said, "Where did that come from?" I told her it had been on the back burner for most of my life. She accepted it. They were a niche publisher, and it became a best seller for them. It won the Whitney Award for Best Historical Novel of 2009!

I have gone on to write over 40 books and am now very comfortable with my voice. As comfortable as when I was a little girl sitting on the floor of my bedroom writing out the tales of Sandy O'Hara.

So, what I wish that I had known sooner was how to unlock my own voice and go forward with it fearlessly. Thank you, Natalie Goldberg. And thank you, Vicki Flake, who passed from this world too soon.

G.G. Vandagriff is the author of over forty novels and an Amazon #1 bestselling author. *The Last Waltz*, the first novel in her 20th Century Historical Romance Series won the Whitney Award for Best Historical Novel in 2009.

GGVandagriff.com

SOFIE RYAN

WRITE WHAT YOU KNOW. Writers have been hearing that advice for a very long time. I wish instead someone had said to me, "Write about the things that intrigue you, the things that snare your attention. Write about what wakes you up in the middle of the night and keeps you awake." You can learn all the things you don't know—how to make a flour bomb, how to choose a guitar, how many number one songs Aerosmith has had. (Surprisingly, just one to date.) You can't learn how to be curious about an idea or a person or a place. You can't learn passion. Those things come from within. Don't write what you know, I would tell my younger self. Write what you love.

Sofie Ryan, *New York Times* bestselling author of the Second Chance Cat Mysteries. Sofie also writes the *New York Times* bestselling Magical Cats Mysteries under the name Sofie Kelly.

SofieKelly.com

VINCENT B. DAVIS II

IF I COULD GO back to an earlier Vincent, I would have so much to tell him. Slow down, enjoy the process, study the craft, make more time for loved ones...

But perhaps more than anything, I would stress the dangers of pride on the writing life. Like many authors, I've always maintained a certain level of pride about my work. Perhaps enamored by my own perceived brilliance, I've always considered my writing with a form of reverence. Since I was a child, I've saved every piece of scrap paper I've ever scribbled a story on, as if one day it might be enshrined to preserve my legacy.

Some might say at least part of this is natural. Authors need a certain form of functional pride to expect others to shell out their hard-earned cash and hours of their life to hear what they have to say.

But over time, and the more and more I've written, I've come to a sobering but comforting realization: it's not about me.

And it never was.

Authors are vessels who serve a very important function. To bring entertainment, escape, and encouragement to our readers. Sometimes this task can get ahead of us, or at least it certainly got ahead of younger Vincent (who am I kidding, it still does).

But our success or failure in this task has never been about our own brilliance. I'm sure you can find more brilliant authors in the cemetery than on the shelves of a Barnes and Noble. That's because our books are not about us. They're about the reader.

It's a subtle distinction, perhaps. One we might be inclined to say, "Well, yeah. Duh." But I see this mistake replicated so often, authors relying on their own importance or the perceived urgency of their message, rather than what exactly they are bringing to their reader's life.

At the end of the day, I don't think the book-buying consumer cares about how brilliant or interesting their author is if they can't deliver a satisfying experience. That's because we, as human beings, care about what we will gain or take away from anything we purchase, even a $3.99 eBook. How will it change us? What will we learn? How might a book— whether it's a self-help book on getting better sleep or a cozy mystery—benefit us in some way?

This shift in perception had a positive impact on me, even if I came to this conclusion later than I might have liked. I stopped worrying about how I might be perceived by the world at large, how I might be remembered after I'm gone. I stopped considering what awards I might win or the talk-shows I might be invited to in a celebration of my success.

Instead, I learned to focus on the experience of my reader. This is baked into the concept and outline of a manuscript, every page of its telling, and in the marketing as well.

Pride has a way of making authors (or at least myself) focus on being the best. As if to be truly great or have any substantial measure of value, we must be the greatest of our time. A literary giant. A *New York Times* bestseller. A Nobel Peace Prize winner.

But I believe the most noble calling an author can have is to write a story which simply gives something to a reader. Anything. As Dean Koontz puts it in *How to Write Best Selling Fiction*, "In a world that encompasses so much pain and fear and cruelty, it is noble to provide a few hours escape, moments of delight and forgetfulness."

If I could go back to a younger Vincent, I'd tell him to stop worrying about being a superstar. Sometimes it's just enough to be a member of the choir.

Vincent B. Davis II is an author, entrepreneur, soldier, a graduate from East Tennessee State University and has served in the United States Army since 2014. He is the author of five books, three of which have become international bestsellers.

VincentBdavisII.com

DIANE KELLY

AS A FORMER CPA and tax advisor, my life was all about numbers before I turned to words instead. Aspiring writers often think of investing their time in their projects, but they don't necessarily think of investing their money in their dream of becoming a published author. They might even feel guilty spending hundreds, if not thousands, of dollars to attend a writers' conference, or even just paying a couple hundred dollars in annual dues to writing organizations. I know. I've been there.

I started writing when my children were in elementary school. Money was somewhat tight then, as I worked only part-time to be home when my kids were out of school. Between dance lessons for our daughter and guitar, bass, and banjo lessons for our son, we were shelling out quite a bit to allow our kids to pursue their passions. I never thought twice about spending money on them, though at times I felt guilty spending money on my own dreams.

Before e-mail submissions became the norm, I spent large amounts on postage sending submissions to agents and editors. I shelled out dues to join several professional writers' organizations, though I had yet to be published. I spent ungodly amounts in gas driving all over the Dallas-Fort Worth metroplex to attend meetings and programs. I spent a small fortune in fees to enter contests sponsored by chapters of Romance Writers of America, hoping to get valuable feedback and to place in the contests so that my work would be seen by the final round judges, who were often agents or editors. I spent another small fortune to attend both national and regional conferences so that I could pitch my projects in person to agents and editors. I felt guilty spending this money on myself … but it paid off! I ended up with offers for my first book from both an editor who had judged my work in an RWA chapter contest and one whom I'd met at an in-person pitch session at a regional conference.

Fortunately, as a tax professional, I knew that I could deduct my writing-related costs as business expenses, so that helped a little with the guilt. I kept meticulous records and took advantage of every allowable deduction. Meals with my critique group. Writing retreats. Supplies. Mileage. I claimed a net loss for years before finally selling my first book and showing a taxable profit.

It's difficult to spend a lot of money on your writing business when there are so many other demands on your budget. Even after getting published and earning some income from work, I balked at buying my first MacBook Air laptop. It seemed like an extravagance when I could buy a PC for one-third the cost. But I bit the bullet and I was so glad I did. The smaller, lightweight MacBook Air computer was much more portable, which works well with my writing style. I tend to move about my house, both indoors and out, as I work. The battery life was much longer, too, which gave me more flexibility. It was a smart decision as it made me much more productive and less distracted. Plus, it was a tax-deductible expense for my writing business.

So, what's the lesson here? YOU are worth investing in. In fact, investing in yourself is the best investment you will ever make. Join organizations that can help you achieve your goals. Network with other writers at meetings and conferences. Buy the supplies and equipment that will make you more productive. Regardless of the monetary return you might achieve, you'll also get an intangible ROI – return on investment – that feeds your spirit and your soul. YOU are worth every cent.

Diane Kelly inadvertently worked with white-collar criminals more than once. Not surprisingly, Diane decided self-employment would be a good idea. Her fingers hit the keyboard and thus began her Death and Taxes romantic mystery series. A graduate of her hometown's Citizen Police Academy, Diane Kelly also writes the hilarious K-9 cop Paw Enforcement series, the Busted female motorcycle cop series, and the House Flipper cozy mystery series. Also, Diane's books have been awarded the prestigious Romance Writers of America Golden Heart® Award and a Reviewers Choice Award.

DianeKelly.com

LISA REGAN

WHAT I WOULD HAVE told my younger writer-self are these things: I would have told myself to spend the money on a freelance content/substantive editor. This would have saved me years of rejections from agents. Also, join a writers' group, even if it is online, and find at least one person—hopefully more—you can exchange work with for critiquing and beta reading purposes. Don't listen to anything family and friends tell you about your work. They will never tell you the truth. Find people who have no emotional stake in your life or your work at all and ask for their unvarnished opinions. All of these things will make you a better writer. Also, your fellow writers will become indispensable and likely very good friends.

It is easier to establish yourself as an author if you choose a genre and stick with it. That's not to say you can't branch out later but it's much easier to find a publisher and a readership if you are consistently writing the same types of things. Readers especially want to know they're getting something they love each time they pick up one of your books. Give them consistency. Imagine if JK Rowling wrote the first Harry Potter book and then, instead of writing more, she'd simply written her crime novel. Readers would be anxiously awaiting the second Harry Potter book and although they might enjoy her crime novel, most probably wouldn't even buy it because it wasn't what they'd hoped for. Instead, she established herself with the Harry Potter franchise and then went on to write her crime novel which was also hugely successful. Although she wrote that under a pen name, I'm sure her agent had no trouble pitching the book to big publishers. Who would turn down the author of the Harry Potter series, regardless of what she wanted to write at that point?

Don't be precious about anything—especially your own work. Develop the ability to ruthlessly cut even your most favorite scenes, chapters, and characters from your work. Just because you think something is awesome doesn't mean it belongs in your book. Always focus on the work itself, not on your personal feelings. Many people will tell you to develop a thick skin, and you should, but you should also develop the ability to divorce your personal feelings from your work entirely so that you can be as objective as possible in making it better. Also don't be afraid to rewrite things entirely. Don't be lazy either. If you can identify an issue with a manuscript and you know that some major rewriting will make it better, then just do that.

Additionally, don't be too precious about covers or anything on the marketing side when it comes to your books. If you want to sell books, then to some degree you need to focus on what readers want and like rather than what you want and like. You might have a cover you love but readers hate or a cover you hate but readers love. Decide what you want. Using the cover example, what do you want? A cover only you love and hardly any sales or a cover you hate but lots of sales. Neither is wrong; you just need to decide what you want. Whether we like it or not, finding readers is part of this business. If you're only writing for your own gratification and you don't care at all whether anyone reads your work, then this doesn't matter, but if you want to sell books and grow a readership then you need to be willing to put your own feelings aside and do what will make your book better and what will get you more readers. James Patterson worked in advertising before he became an author and in his Masterclass, he talks about outlines for his books in terms of how scenes and the plot will make readers feel. You have to take readers into account if you want to sell books.

Keep creating new content. This is the key to a long career, in my opinion. A very select few authors see their debut novels shoot straight to the top of every bestseller list and become worldwide sensations. That's wonderful when it happens, but don't count on it. If you want to grow readership, keep creating new content. If you've got some readers, but you want more, keep creating new content. It wasn't until my sixth book that my career started to take off in a major way. I personally loved my first five books, and I wish that many more readers would have as well, but they just didn't. Instead of trying to push books that had already been published to mediocre sales, I kept writing. Writing more books won't guarantee success but it certainly increases your chances. Plus, if one of your newer books suddenly becomes very successful, all the books on your backlist will get a nice boost in readership and sales.

There's only one correct way to write a book: the way that works best for you. You're going to hear tons of advice about how to write a book. If none of those ways of writing a book works for you, don't be alarmed. Everyone's process is different, and that's okay. Figure out what your process is and lean into it. I took Becca Syme's online class, Write Better Faster, to figure out what my writing process was and it revolutionized the way I wrote. I wish I had taken it before I even wrote my first novel. It would have saved me years of heartache and inefficient writing.

Finally, don't compare yourself to others, just try to make your next book better than your last.

Lisa Regan is the *USA Today* & *Wall Street Journal* bestselling author of the Detective Josie Quinn series as well as several other crime fiction titles.

LisaRegan.com

JUSTIN LESLIE

AS AN AUTHOR, I like to tell tales. I often tell people you can believe as much as you think I'm willing to tell when it comes to my story. To date, I have written twelve books and produced ten best-selling audiobooks. The one and only Luke Daniels performs the Max Abaddon Series. Even more pressing has been doing this over a span of twenty four months as a currently independent author. What could possibly go wrong?

The two main series I currently write are the Max Abaddon Series, Urban Fantasy stuff, and The Sinking Man Series, Zombie stuff. I'm not counting the space opera I have half-written sitting in a dusty computer folder.

A long and surprising path led me to become an author. I joined the army at eighteen and was able to retire after several long years. The odd thing about traveling around the world and having time to do things like read was I found myself devouring entire series. Plus, I needed the escape.

Before long, I had ripped through most of the major series in the urban fantasy genre (think Harry Potter for grown-ups). Authors such as Jim Butcher, Patricia Briggs, and Kevin Hearne, to name a few. What eventually became clear was I had somehow become somewhat of an expert in the UF genre. I eventually started branching out to the indie titles and quickly learned that people were out in the world self-publishing books.

Needless to say, after a night of rather questionable cheap whiskey and some time in my office behind the computer, I had typed out the first chapter in what would become the Max Abaddon Series. There was of course, a motivation in me doing so.

One thing I have strived for as a successful author is to not fall into the typical indie, or traditionally published cooker cutter, cut and paste novel. This was the trap, and I noticed the frequency of those books available for readers. Most of the authors I associate myself with are bucking the system and putting out some of the freshest new material out there for the genres I write in.

With both my current series, I have strived to bring something fresh to both the genres I write in. The Sinking Man Series is a different point of view on how to approach the zombie apocalypse. Ever wonder what it would be like to actually be prepared? I have plans for the series to get picked up for TV in the near future. Jarrett Lemaster, the actor, performs that series and is amazing! I recommend keeping an eye out for his work.

The Max Abaddon Series follows Max on his journey as the magical world comes out to the rest of society. He also likes to get into trouble.

I always like to think I started my journey as a professional writer with several lessons learned, or as they are rightfully called failures. As a master's degree toting author, there was a time when I started that I assumed I could do no wrong with my grammar. Five editors, dozens of poor reviews, and well over $7K later, I had experienced my first true failure. While I was selling books, I was losing the initial audience that I had worked hard to reach.

Of course, as with most lessons, there was a silver lining here. I was initially simply looking for someone to magically fix what I had written. When you are writing ninety-thousand-word novels, things like spelling and proper sentence structure can take a sideline.

I had fallen into the old I-know-better trap. On several occasions, other authors I know stated that a good editor is worth their weight in gold. This one learned truth ended up steering the rest of my choices throughout my writing career and also taught me an invaluable lesson.

In the writing industry, where self-publication is quickly becoming the standard, finding true partnerships with vendors and supportive networks such as cover designers, editors, and audiobook narrators is a must.

The old adage 'you get what you pay for' is the exact advice I give to newer authors seeking guidance.

Another major takeaway on the path to becoming a successful author is just how helpful and cool other authors are. Not only do you have similar tastes, but in most cases, similar goals. I have made friends that I will stay in contact with and support for years to come. When I first started my journey, I did the typical 'I'm a google expert' type of research. Hours of YouTube and everything in between.

Then one day, instead of reading how-tos online, I went to my favorite authors' webpages and started reading their bios. At the end of it, I simply hit the contact button, not thinking I would hear back when I suddenly got flooded with responses from some of my favorite authors eager to answer my questions. This knowledge set me on the right path. It's odd being the one that gets these emails now.

From there, I ended up getting through my first novel to again being linked up with a great author when I started my audiobook journey. Something I think will continue to grow. Hunter Blain, author of the Preternatural Chronicles (the most unique new vampire series out) really went out of his way to help me here.

With that all said, I used to tell my soldiers when I was a light Infantry commander a very simple bit of advice. "Get a mentor, even if they don't fit the mold or are like you. Find someone who's work and drive you respect."

Justin S. Leslie is a fervent urban fantasy fan and bestselling author. When he isn't writing, playing music or spending time with his wife and two boys, he can be found at his Doctors Inlet home, immersed in the latest urban fantasy, or a well-made cocktail.

JustinLeslie.com

NANCY COCO

GOSH, IF I COULD go back to that 5th grader who wanted to write a book. That 14-year-old who whipped out short stories left and right. That 20-year-old who wanted to write an entire (500 page) novel before she turned 21. That 35-year-old who had already written 12 novels, had three agents and had yet to sell anything. What could I tell them? What word of advice would help, would not make it all seem futile, would not sound trite?

I guess that advice would be stop comparing yourself, your writing, your journey to others. The world loves to talk about the lottery winners. The ones who sell their first book. Who after three books make the NYT bestseller list. The ones with legions of fans and fairytale money. Those who make movies or ongoing television series. Those who win the Booker Award, the Pulitzer, an Oscar, a Nobel prize.

That may or may not be your journey, but it doesn't make your journey any less important. There are thousands who write one book and are done. That is their journey and that's okay. Thousands who toil daily and never make more than a thousand dollars, five thousand dollars, a few hundred. Others who pound out hundreds of books that delight their readers. Whatever turns out to happen is your journey. Readers will love you, or hate you, or ignore you and sometimes all three. But none of that matters. What matters is your personal journey through craft, the friendships you build, the people who connect with your stories, your art.

You are successful just by trying and by doing.

Then I would say, find a coach. There are good writing coaches out there whether they are teachers, mentors, authors. Find a coach and listen to their advice. But be careful. When you rely too heavily on other's points of view, you lose your voice, and it is your voice that is needed in the work that you do. You can't be the next Patterson, Twain, Angelou, but you can be the first you.

Be brave. Don't hide your work. You can't get read if the book never sees the light of day. You can't get better if you don't ask someone to tell you what they think. But most importantly, trust your gut. This is your journey. Your path. Go and follow it.

USA Today bestselling author, Nancy Coco enjoys a good mystery. She is lucky enough to indulge her love of a good who dunnit by writing mystery series. Fun settings, quirky characters, yummy recipes and pets of all shapes and sizes fill the pages of her multiple, award-winning series. Nancy writes as Nancy J Parra, Nancy Coco and Nell Hampton.

NancyJCoco.com

KRISTEN LUCIANI

"DEATH INSPIRES ME LIKE a dog inspires a rabbit."

First, let me just say…this quote, while brilliant, isn't mine. It's a lyric that belongs to the band Twenty One Pilots. I'll admit, when I first heard it, I scratched my head. I did that the next five times I heard it, too.

Is it about a dog? Is it about dying? How the heck did a rabbit get pulled into the mix?

But then, I actually considered the deeper meaning hidden behind these words. To me, this quote is all about drive, passion, and motivation. Fear of the unknown is common. Fear of failure can prevent us from heading down a potentially lucrative and rewarding path. We would rather miss out on opportunities, fearing the worst outcome may occur. Hitting the brick wall when our path ends abruptly because we were too afraid to persevere is *death* in a metaphorical sense.

I refuse to hit that wall. I do everything in my power to circumvent it, crash through it, leap over it…whatever will eliminate the possibility that my plans will come to a screeching halt.

That means I need to accept and embrace the possibility of failure.

Failure is actually a good thing. It helps us to learn and grow in whatever discipline we pursue.

So how do you wander into a brand-new venture while limiting the potential for failure?

Over time and through plenty of gut-wrenching experience, I stumbled upon something that can save you tremendous amounts of time, money, and energy.

Research.

Research is one of the keys to success in any endeavor, and that's a hard lesson I learned many years before I delved into my author career.

Back in 2005, I launched a handbag design business. I didn't have a background in fashion and had no idea how to navigate the accessories market. The biggest driver behind my decision was that I loved handbags. I wanted to create the next "it" handbag that would be embraced by celebrities and fashionistas. So, being the impulsive and instant gratification person that I am, I designed a boatload of handbags, found a manufacturer in Manhattan, and produced my first line.

I never talked to a single person in my target market before risking tens of thousands of dollars on my products. I didn't have any confirmation that my handbags would meet the needs and expectations of buyers.

So much money. So much heartbreak. So much frustration.

And it was all because I didn't do a stitch of research before throwing myself head first into the venture. Research applies to all aspects of a new venture, from craft to marketing and through to networking and promotion.

When I wrote my first book, I had no idea how to create a story arc. I didn't know that you're not supposed to do backstory dumps in the beginning of your books. I was clueless about the concept of "show, don't tell."

I also didn't know anything about the indie publishing industry. I focused on writing and tried to develop my skills in that capacity. I knew nothing of sub-genres, tropes, or social media promotion. I didn't have a website. I didn't belong to any Facebook author groups. I didn't realize there was a raging book blogger world in existence.

I never took the time to do the appropriate research about how to market a book. I figured readers would magically find it on Amazon and one-click it because it had such a unique cover. That was another pitfall I fell into...thinking that being unique was the golden ticket.

No research!

Amazon is an amazing research tool. You can evaluate the best seller lists and look at covers and blurbs to determine common elements shared by each trope or genre. I did that but instead of considering the common elements for my own cover, I went in the exact opposite direction so I'd stand out from the crowd.

I didn't realize standing out was a bad thing.

When you create a cover that doesn't resonate with readers, no matter how amazing it is, they won't one-click your book. You need to let readers know when they click on your product page exactly what they will find within the pages of your book. My book cover screamed a genre, but it wasn't the one I'd written.

Suffice to say that throughout my author career I made a lot of expensive mistakes, all because I didn't do the appropriate research. I know I sound like a broken record by now but trust me, the rewards will be well worth the time you will spend understanding the industry before you hit the "publish" button on your screen.

Know your competition before you jump into this industry. Study trends, read articles, reach out to other authors for their insights, and form a mastermind group so that you can grow with others. Talk to readers, understand their buying patterns, learn about their expectations and how to satisfy them in your stories.

It is extremely rare to accidentally fall into greatness. You need to create a solid strategy and plan for achieving excellence. Then execute, rinse, and repeat!

Kristen Luciani, *USA Today* bestselling author of dark, dangerous, and deliciously sexy romance.

KirstenLuciani.com

JULIE ANNE LINDSEY

I WISH I WOULD'VE known years sooner that it's okay to say no. And I wish I would've said no more often. A LOT more often.

Something we don't talk about often enough in this industry is the unrelenting pressure put on creatives to be creative— AROUND THE CLOCK. We're told to grow our network, to increase our platform, to attend events and create a brand long before we've ever finished our first book. We're also told to read, write, and hone our craft, but don't forget to establish ourselves on social media, interact with the online community, be witty and fun. Become relevant. Write posts. Guest blog for others. Accept interviews, and to seek them too! Contact podcasters. Email reviewers. Reach out to influencers. To booktubers. Join Tik Tok! Talk to book clubs, speak at libraries, and get to know your local bookstores. Host online events. Have a book launch party! Teach classes. Take classes. Do a giveaway. Create a reader group. Write articles. Send them to websites and magazines. And remember— you have to write the very best book you can if you want to stand out in this crowded marketplace.

Whatever you do, keep adding more tasks to your list until you can't breathe.

Until there's no more time for yourself.

Or your family.

Or to write.

While we're spinning like weary tops, we're told that if we dare say no to whatever is asked of us, someone else will say yes. And the next time an opportunity arises, everyone will remember we once said no, and we won't be asked again.

We're told that if we don't do EVERYTHING, that will be the reason we fail.

I wish I'd have known at the start of my career that this pressure is false. Contrived. Made up by people who either have no idea what it takes to get published and be successful, or by those angling to get something from you — like free blog material and workshop content.

As a new or aspiring author, your only job is to write the best book you can and to make sure your readers know they're appreciated. You do that by taking care of yourself and pursuing those things that bring you joy. Say no to the things that don't either make you happy or further your career in an actual way. Or come with payment for services as jobs should.

In other words, if you've got time to give the blogger in your inbox a top five list of ways to kill a fictional character at Christmas, and you want to do it, great! But if you just don't have time, or the desire, say no. And don't feel guilty about it.

Tell people your schedule is too full.

Tell people to try you again in the spring. (Or fall, or never, because what they want isn't the kind of thing you typically do.)

Tell your readers when you need a break.

Give yourself permission to say no. And thank folks for thinking of you anyway.

Rest and refuel your creative heart and mind.

And do not feel guilty.

Julie Anne Lindsey is an award-winning and bestselling author of mystery and romantic suspense. She's published more than fifty novels since her debut in 2013 and currently writes series as herself, as well as under multiple pen names, Bree Baker, Jacqueline Frost, Julie Chase, for Harlequin, Kensington, Sourcebooks and Crooked Lane Books.

JulieAnneLindsay.com

PERSISTENCE

*"Nothing in the world can take the place of persistence. Talent
will not; nothing is more common than unsuccessful men
with talent. Genius will not; unrewarded genius is almost
a proverb. Education will not; the world is full of educated
derelicts. Persistence and determination alone are omnipotent.
The slogan Press On! has solved and always will solve the
problems of the human race."*

— Calvin Coolidge

M.D. MASSEY

WHEN I WAS ASKED to contribute to this work, I didn't have to think long about the advice I would offer to new and aspiring authors. Writers approach me seeking advice all the time. Because I remember what it was like when I was starting out, I'm always happy to provide insights into what it takes to become a successful professional indie author.

Let's jump right in...

Defining Success

I believe that before one embarks on a new undertaking, it's prudent to define some goals first. Since the goal of many aspiring authors is to achieve "success," we should define that term for ourselves when we begin to pursue a career as an author.

Think for a moment about what success as an author means to you. Does it mean getting a publishing contract (hybrid is the way many indie authors choose to go, after all)? Would it mean hitting a bestseller list? Selling one-hundred-thousand, or even a million, copies? Replacing your current income with your book royalties? Retiring your spouse from work?

I could go on and on. However, we're talking about your goals here, not mine. As such, I would encourage you to spend some time examining your goals and dreams to determine what precisely you want to achieve in your career. Whatever you settle on, make a list and write your goals down—trust me on that part.

Luck vs. Work

First, let's discuss the element of "chance" as it applies to becoming a successful indie author. I don't believe in luck, necessarily, but I do believe it's possible to do everything right while still failing to make it as a full-time author. For proof, all you need to do is look at all the talented authors who aren't selling books on Amazon.

It's undeniable that some authors succeed despite a lack of knowledge regarding the business side of things. Many successful authors will readily admit that they don't understand advertising, branding, platform, or any of the other elements of marketing oneself as an author that are considered de rigueur in the indie publishing industry.

Yet, we see such authors succeeding on a regular basis. The common refrain heard when examining and discussing these outliers is that they wrote books that readers wanted to read. But is that enough?

Anyone who has been in this industry long enough will tell you it isn't. There are plenty of talented authors out there who can pen an entertaining yarn—and most of them are languishing in obscurity, unpublished, unbought, unseen. So, what is it that allows some authors to succeed while others do not?

Taking outliers into account, we must assume that there is a certain element of chance involved in whether or not an author will succeed. I would say that it's more a matter of timing than chance in some cases, but certainly chance is clearly a factor in the careers of many well-known, full-time authors.

That said, *do not let this discourage you.* This is because, for those of us who are less fortunate regarding the hand we've been dealt, there's always a way to compensate.

The Harder I Work...

It was Coleman Cox who first said, "I am a great believer in luck. The harder I work, the more of it I seem to have." He was right.

One factor that can be observed among the majority of successful indie authors is the quality of being prolific. Successful indie authors—meaning, those who enjoy lasting, satisfying careers— are hard workers. They write, and many of them write thousands of words every single day.

If we accept that the element of "chance" is a factor in our success as an indie author, then wouldn't we want to stack the deck in our own favor? Consider that every good book we publish is another time our name is dropped in the hat, another lottery ticket, another opportunity for our work to be enjoyed and shared by enthusiastic readers.

Notice I said, "shared." When book lovers find a novel they love, they tend to share it. Of course, that's why studying the craft is so important to us as authors, but it's also why we want to get as many books published as possible. More books, more chances that readers will become fans of our work.

So, write. Write every day, edit what you write, hire a professional editor to edit what you have edited, and then get that book published. Rinse and repeat, refining your craft and process each and every time. This is how indie author careers are made.

The Virtues of Being Stubborn

It's been said that goals are dreams with a deadline, but we all know that not everyone completes their plans on time. While we may set out with a goal of going full-time within a year, or two years, or what have you, that deadline may very well pass us by before our goal is achieved.

That's why we need to be stubborn about pursuing our goals. Often the difference between authors who make it and authors who don't is simply persistence. If you really want to become a successful full-time author, then you must be willing to continue writing and publishing your work until your goal is met.

It was six years from the date I published my first novel to the time I became a full-time author. Prior to the publication of my first novel, I'd spent another four years writing a half-dozen unfinished novels, reading books on writing, taking writing courses, studying the craft, and honing my skills as an author.

That's ten years of toiling away at the keyboard, never really sure of whether or not I was wasting my time from a financial perspective.

Certainly, none of that time was wasted. Looking back, it was time well spent indeed. The decade I spent learning the craft and business of writing and publishing resulted in the achievement of a dream I'd had since I was a child.

Stick with it. Keep writing. Polish, then publish your work. Then do it again. Whether in one year or ten, it will pay off.

M.D. Massey's eclectic background provides him with a rich tapestry of experiences to draw on when crafting fiction, as evidenced by the believable worlds and relatable characters he creates.

MDMassey.com

PAUL HEATLEY

EDITING IS IMPORTANT.

The worst thing a writer can believe is that they're inherently talented. Perhaps someone told them they were good at writing – that they have a *talent* for it. If you have a talent, surely you don't need to worry much about editing. That talent will just shine right off the page. And then, long-term, if you fall out of writing, don't keep up the practice, it's fine, because you're *talented*.

But then, as the rejections mount up, you start to doubt that this is true. You might lose any belief you have that you're talented. Maybe you never were. Maybe you've got nothing to offer. Maybe you're just not meant to be a writer.

I started writing when I was young. Nothing serious. Bits and pieces here and there, pen and paper. In high school, when I was thirteen, soon to be fourteen, we got our first computer. I would write on it every night after school. I'd write truly awful horror stories and send them to short story magazines and I never got a thing published. Those stories, though I don't really remember them, I wonder sometimes if they really were as bad as I think. Perhaps there was a good idea in there somewhere. Perhaps under all that overwritten, poorly written, adjective-laden rubbish, there could have been something worth salvaging. My method of editing at that time was one quick proof-read and then to send it off. That wasn't an edit, not really. It's not surprising I didn't get anything published.

There's a video on YouTube, on a channel called Big Think. 'Henry Rollins: The One Decision That Changed My Life Forever.' It's seven minutes and six seconds long, and it's the most important thing I've ever watched. There is a line that, when I first heard it ten years ago, it resounded for me, and I have repeated it to myself every day since: "I don't have talent, I have tenacity."

If you want to be a writer, you can't give up. If you doubt your talent, or believe you don't have any, that's fine, so long as you don't give up. Swap talent for tenacity any day of the week.

There's another line in the video. It's not as neat an aphorism as the one above, and it's part of a larger point he's making, but I've condensed down the important part, the part that hit home to me: "Other people might have to write something once, but I have to write it three times."

I watched that video, and that's when I got serious. I'd write a story and I'd edit it not once, or twice, but three, four, five, sometimes six times. Maybe more, if it needed it. I'd read and edit it until it was burned onto my eyeballs.

Then something started to happen.

The rejections became acceptances. A lot of acceptances. Because I was finally putting in the work, day after day, and I was doing it properly. Getting the words down on paper isn't enough. They have to be done right. They have to be edited, sometimes over and over and over again. No one else is going to do it for me. No one has the time, or the patience, or the interest, to fix something if I send it to them half-baked. The only person that cares is me, and I have to treat each story, each novel, each sentence, accordingly.

So what I wish I'd known, way back when I started writing, was the harsh truth: I'm not talented. But that's fine, because I can always be something much better: tenacious.

Paul Heatley is the author of the Tom Rollins series of books, as well as several standalone titles and more than fifty short stories. He lives in the north east of England.

PaulHeatley.com

MELINDA WOODHALL

I WISH SOMEONE HAD told me that timing would be key when it came to building my writing career.

I turned to writing novels after two decades of telling myself I was too busy raising a family and working sixty hours a week to ever have the time. Looking back from my new vantage point as a full-time writer of dozens of novels, I can see in hindsight that I was exactly right.

There was no need for me to regret "all those wasted years" that passed by without a finished (or even started) novel since I truly didn't have the time, energy, life experience, financial means, or mental focus needed to write and promote long- form fiction…at least not then.

If nothing else, writing novels takes loads and loads of time. And that means sacrificing other activities and priorities to make room for writing. As a young working mother, I under-standably wasn't prepared to do that, and am now grateful I devoted myself to my young family and to building a stable financial foundation. The right time to devote myself to writing would come later.

Through the years I never let my dream slip away. When the timing was right, I made space in my life to write. Time to think and plan and dream. And with much contemplation and musing I began to write stories using experiences, knowledge, and ideas which had ripened and flourished over the years and were finally ready to bear fruit.

Melinda Woodhall is the author of over twenty heart-stopping thrillers, including the Mercy Harbor Thriller series, Veronica Lee Thriller series, and Bridget Bishop FBI Mystery Thriller series.

MelindaWoodhall.com

NAZRI NOOR

I WOULD HAVE TOLD myself to build a thicker skin, and to cultivate grit. Call it persistence, call it tenacity, whatever you like. Some of the most successful indies didn't take off immediately with their first series, instead attracting their core readership somewhere around the second.

And that's perfectly fine. Some authors come out the gate with a single release and make a killing with just the one book. For others, the hit comes later down the line. And unless you're among the chosen, trust that there will be flops. That's where the thick skin comes in.

But failure is just a learning opportunity. Publishing in my experience is a game of iterating and refining the process. Every book is another chance to try something new, improve your craft, practice everything you've learned about how to tell a riveting story.

Because that's what we're all hoping to do at the end of the day, isn't it? Climb onto the highest tower and shout out the very best story you can tell, to as many people who will listen.

Some authors are content with the satisfaction of having written. I'd be lying if I said I was one of them. Don't feel terribly about wanting to earn a living with your art. You deserve to earn a living with your art. You don't have to be a bestseller, either. It's entirely possible to make a comfortable living on the midlist.

So keep writing. Make yourself heard. Then write again, and again, until your fingers give out or the universe collapses. Whichever comes first.

Nazri Noor, independent fantasy and romance author of over 30 novels.

NazriNoor.com

ELIZABETH PENNEY

OVER TWO DECADES AGO, I was part of a wonderful on-line group called the Mystery's Writer's Forum. How long it takes to get published was a frequent topic of discussion. One commenter said it could take twenty years of trying.

Why did I feel a twinge in my gut as if the bell of doom had tolled? I just knew that was going to be me. And it was. In 2019, my first traditionally published mystery was released by St. Martin's Press.

Lest I exhaust you, it wasn't a straight twenty years of constant effort. At the time I decided to try writing fiction seriously, I was a wife and mother, business consultant and MBA student. I owned an Aladdin kit house, two cats and a dog, and was active in my local community. My skill set was more on the finance and analysis side, but my college English professor told me I should be a writer. My secret dream, ever since I started checking out books in a very old library in Maine.

Hold on. My professor suggested I become a *writer*, based on my papers for his class on the Transcendentalists. The art and craft of writing encompasses much, much, much more than the narrow definition of fiction published with an agent and a trad deal. My career helping small businesses offered me opportunities to write. Instructive case studies. Editing and writing for a statewide business newspaper. Articles published by a variety of well-regarded publications.

So, I wrote anything I could in between working on books and sending out submissions, and then, later queries to agents. Along the way, I had two that didn't work out and I also turned down two book deals. That's right. I said no.

Believe me, sometimes by the time you get an offer, you're so desperate to finally grab the brass ring you'll take any chance to break through. *But.* Remember that business education? Contracts are key. What do those clauses and terms mean? Sorry to tell you this, it's your responsibility to know and understand them. Even if you have an agent. Even a good one who is savvy at negotiating and explaining down-the-road consequences to you.

Both companies have since ceased publishing the genres I subbed. Yeah. My books would now be dead in the water, with only the first in a series released.

Another opportunity I stumbled upon and grabbed with both hands was writing for subscription book clubs. These are multi-author series and work-for-hire, a whole other big world of writing. While I continued to seek—and sometimes temporarily give up—my trad dream, I wrote dozens of books for these wonderful publishers. Although I was working in their series world, I learned so much about every aspect of fiction writing.

Even sweeter, the experience I had gained meant I could submit on proposal. (one of the most frustrating and difficult aspects of the trad route is the requirement to write *whole books*—maybe over and over again. Who has that much time?) So to summarize, after twenty years of effort, when *it finally happened*, it took *two weeks* to get *multiple offers* on my *proposal.*

So—what do I wish I'd known? That, yes, it would take a very long time. And that it would be okay. Along the way I became a pro writer—with a multi-faceted career.

Elizabeth Penney, author of more than three dozen mystery, women's fiction, and romantic suspense titles, including the Edgar-nominated *Chapter and Curse*, first in the Cambridge Bookshop series.

ElizabethPenneyAuthor.com

CHRISTOPHER MITCHELL

EVERY WRITER FACES A different journey, but there exists a similar core of attributes shared by any who succeed. By 'succeed,' I do not necessarily mean acquiring fame or riches – the goals set out by each writer are personal to them. For some, it might be to finish drafting the book they have been dreaming about for years; while for others, it might be to publish something critically acclaimed – but, regardless of the goal, success requires certain qualities that anyone can possess.

1. Persistence. The simplest advice to my younger self can be summed up in two words – keep writing. Persist, on the bad days as well as the good. Make writing a habit; force yourself into the chair, even if you can't be bothered – especially if you can't be bothered. Only through continual practice will a writer find and develop their voice. There are no short-cuts. Like a new pilot who needs to accumulate hours in the sky, new writers have to build up their hours spent writing.

2. Self-Belief. This is the quality that will see you through the bad days. Believe in yourself. This doesn't mean that you should imagine yourself to be the greatest writer who has ever existed. Any such notions will only prove to be so brittle that they will shatter at

the first hurdle. Instead, believe in what you are doing, and believe that you are good enough to do it well. Believe that you are capable of improvement. Anyone who keeps writing will find that their style gets better over time, and that their mistakes lessen. Don't be disheartened if your first attempts seem poor or unworthy – first drafts are a necessary step towards improvement, and every writer goes through this process. No one arrives fully-formed.

3. Develop a thick skin. Writers reveal their vulnerabilities to the world. For some writers, their characters feel alive, and their books can seem almost as precious as children. Just as no parent likes to hear criticism aimed at their child, it is possible for some writers to develop a fragile sense of ego. Harsh words directed at a piece of work that has been sweated and agonized over can cut like a knife. Understand that you will never please everyone. No matter how proficient and skilled a writer may be, there will always be someone who dislikes, or even hates, your work; and in the age of the internet, these voices can break through, in the form of bad reviews, in emails of complaint, or through hurtful comments on social media. Cherish the good reviews, and ignore the bad. Learn to discriminate between constructive criticism, which should be welcomed, and petty barbs, which should be ignored. This is easier said than done, of course.

4. Own it. If you are writing, then you are a writer.

Own that simple fact. You are not an 'aspiring' writer, you are a writer, full stop. Never be ashamed or embarrassed about this. Never cringe if you write 'genre' fiction, such as romance or science fiction/fantasy, and someone asks what you do. Writing works that entertain readers is a noble profession. Writers can make people laugh, cry and think; and for many, a good book is a source of great comfort that can tide people through dark times in their lives. Be proud of this fact. Own it.

Christopher Mitchell is the author of the epic fantasy series the Magelands.

ChristopherMitchellBooks.com

RICK JONES

JUST LIKE IT TAKES a village to raise a child, it takes many people to create a good novel. But the author is always the one who aspires to bring their story to light. So, the ambition to write is always there until frustration sets in. First, learn the craft of writing by reading novels of whatever genre you want to specialize in to get a feel of the building and development, and how to flesh out characters. With having a reasonable understanding of the fundamental basics of writing a novel, do so knowing that getting published by a traditional publisher is difficult and that earning enough money to support your dream job as a novelist is even more difficult to achieve, though not impossible given the indie route. Remember, the word 'impossible' does not mean that something cannot be done, it simply measures the degree of difficulty. Now with indie platforms such as Amazon, Barnes & Noble, etc., it's easy to publish your book. However, make sure that it's the best possible product since first impressions are everything to a reader. If there are misspellings, pasteboard characters, or grammatical issues, then your second novel is already dead in the water since it's unlikely that your audience will return to read future volumes. It is imperative that you don't pen a rehash of what's already been written. Find something novel and unique. **Secondly, have your work edited by a professional!** This is paramount. Once you forge and hammer out a story with well-developed characters and conflict, once you're sure that the book is finely tuned grammatically, then you have the choice of submitting to an agent or self-pub.

Good luck on the former since most agents rarely respond if at all. If you choose to self-pub, then keep in mind that you'll need to become an expert at self-marketing. Go online and find groups that help each other promote their works. But most of all, never give up. It took me thirty-two years to achieve success. With today's e-platforms and the ability to self-pub as I did, I was finally able to grab the brass ring of success. I've accomplished the sales of more than 500,000 ebooks. My line was picked up by a traditional publisher in Europe with sales skyrocketing on the international market. And I've been signed to a TV contract with my books currently in global development with a very prominent executive producer. So, my advice is this: Don't quit. In the end, your determination and perseverance will get you there all the time.

Rick Jones is the national and international bestselling novelist of the Vatican Nights series, which is in global development to become a TV series through Executive Producer Ileen Maisel of Amber Entertainment (Dangerous Liaisons, The Golden Compass, The Star Chamber, Romeo and Juliet).

RickJonz.com

KIERSTEN MODGLIN

WHEN I STARTED OUT, I thought (like so many writers do) my first book would be this smashing success. I remember counting out how many copies I'd need to sell to retire, already imagining the lavish vacations I'd be able to take my family on. Unfortunately, that didn't happen. And, I think most writers need to understand how *very rare* it is for that to happen. You probably won't be traveling the world on your private jet being asked for autographs after your debut novel. Most days, you'll feel like you're shouting into the void, just hoping someone will hear you and take a chance on your work. Sorry to be the bearer of bad news, but trust me, I should know. I didn't "break out" with my first book, my second, or even my tenth. In fact, it wasn't until my thirteenth book that I found some semblance of success. By my fifteenth novel, I was able to retire from my day job. And with my seventeenth novel, I retired my husband and we finally took that vacation. I know some writers who've found success much earlier in their journeys than I did and some writers who've been working for much longer than I have and they still aren't where they want to be. When you're in the early days of your publishing career, I think it's important to understand that so much of what you'll be doing is purely for the love of it. I've been writing since I was very young, and I'd still be writing now even if I hadn't reached some of my early goals. I often joke that if things hadn't worked out like they have for me, I would've gladly been ninety years old releasing my two hundredth book believing *this* one will be the one to finally make the difference. I wouldn't have given up simply because I *couldn't*. I don't know how to *not be writing*. Even if I never published another book, I'd be at my keyboard tomorrow just for me. It's important to know that in the beginning. To know yourself. To manage your expectations. Very few writers find success after just one or two books. Most of us have to wake up every day and continue to make our way up the mountain until the stars align. There will be setbacks and landslides and sometimes, you'll think you've finally reached the peak just to look ahead and realize there's so much farther to climb. So, my advice to all writers starting out is simple: Write the book. Release it. Market it with every ounce of energy you have. All the while, be writing your next one. And your next. And your next. Write and release. There's no reason to wait for your first book to do well before working on your next one. Each new book is a chance to reach a handful of new readers. Think of it as if each time a reader needs to choose what to read next, they're drawing a name from a hat—the more slips of paper your name appears on, the more likely each reader will be to draw your name. Just keep writing and releasing, believing in yourself, clawing to find each and every reader, appreciating the ones you do have, enjoying every moment of it, and knowing that you will keep going with no guarantee you'll ever reach your definition of success. That's the key. Persistence and an absolute love for this career. You'll need both to find happiness on this path we've chosen. You'll need both to keep returning back to the keyboard. This isn't a get-rich-quick scheme or an easy career, but if you love it, every trek up the mountain, every name written on a slip of paper, and every single day shouting into the void will be worth it."

Kiersten Modglin, KDP All-Star and Amazon Top 30 bestselling author of more than 30 award-winning

psychological thrillers with over half a million copies
sold worldwide.

www.KierstenModglinAuthor.com

ROSS GREENWOOD

SINCE I'VE BEEN WRITING, I've been asked many times how I do it, or what advice I'd give, and I generally say the same thing. Pick up a pen, write chapter one, and you're off. You're a writer now. I think that's the only way. Obviously, it's unlikely you'll do that, because I didn't. Few authors do.

You'll probably have an idea bubbling away in your head that talks to you in the bath or when you're walking the dog. You'll doubt anyone would be interested in your story. So you don't bother starting it, and you'll be slightly relieved that you can now forget this stupid idea.

But the characters don't go away. They appear when you're ironing, or first thing in the morning when you wake. Deep down you'll know that, many years from now, on your deathbed, it's unlikely you're going to say to yourself, I'm glad I didn't write that book.

As time goes by, the main protagonists in your book will flesh out in your head. You'll imagine how they'll react to certain situations. You'll probably be able to picture them, because it's likely that one of the characters is you.

That's right. Many first novels are semi-autobiographical. It might be a subconscious itch to write your own story. My first novel was very much like that. The main character was me. I was lucky enough to read some advice before I got started that said don't fall into the trap of thinking your life story is interesting. It probably isn't interesting enough.

That's also true. You'll read a lot before you get started. The internet is full of advice, but as Baz Luhrmann said, "Advice is a form of nostalgia: dispensing it is a way of fishing the past from the disposal, wiping it off, painting over the ugly parts, and recycling it for more than it's worth." Nevertheless, you'll read tonnes of it before getting started in the same way when you were studying for your exams at school, you would find yourself doing anything but, even reading the back of cereal boxes.

The great thing is at this point in your writing career, because trust me, you've already started on that career, you'll realise that there are no boundaries. You can still write your story that's a bit about you, but you can make yourself taller, richer, more murderous, or whatever you can imagine.

In some ways, that first book will be your best book, but it will also be your worst. It will be great, because it will have been circulating in your head in one form or another for years, maybe even decades, but it won't be brilliant, because you won't really know what you're doing.

That's part of the fun. It's a strangely emotional experience when you decide to get started. One good piece of advice is that when you do get started, commit to finishing it. Tell yourself, I will do this, and you will.

It won't be easy. In every book until my seventh, I had what I call the 20,000-word wobble. At that point, I'd think that it sucked. It doesn't. Drive on my friend, even if you only manage a hundred words that day.

Even if you get to the end of your first novel and decide to lob it in a drawer, you'll never be short of a talking point at parties in the future. In fact, do lob it in a drawer when you've finished. Leave it for at least a month. When you get it out, I guarantee that you will be surprised by it. You do have talent, after all. Probably more than you hoped for.

When you write The End, and you will if you commit to it, you will look around in excitement. You'll need to tell someone! It's a wonderful feeling. You'll be surprised when most of your family aren't as excited as you are. Some will be jealous, though.

There is much advice on the internet about getting your work published. It's not easy. I suggest you join a writer's group on Facebook, like UK Crime Book Club if you write crime, and bare your soul. They are very friendly and inclusive, and the writers in the group will all have been where you are on your journey. They are your best source of advice at this stage of your journey. You'll make friends. Offer to read another aspiring author's work for them and they will return the favour. You can never have too many people give you feedback on your efforts.

Finally, enjoy it. Why do it otherwise? Celebrate every success, because there will be dips. Your first bad review will really suck, and you'll remember it long after you forget your first fabulous review. But, once you've sobered up, you might find a few specks of good advice within that review. You can always kill them in your next book.

Your writing will improve. Success is unlikely to come overnight. Many an author will tell you it took five years to become an overnight success. It wasn't until I wrote my sixth book that I made any proper progress.

One of the reasons it's so hard to make money nowadays is because of the sheer volume of published material. In years past, your book would have been on the bookshelves until it stopped selling, then the bookstore would have sent the remainder back to the publisher to be pulped or flogged in Poundland. Nowadays, with kindle and print on demand, your book will probably be around on Amazon for eternity, forever competing against Moby Dick and Wuthering Heights.

Perhaps it will be something your great grandchildren will read many years in the future. Remember, your first novel tends to be semi-autobiographical, so that gives them a little chance to learn about their ancestors from times gone by. You can give your own advice from beyond the grave. So get started. What more motivation do you need?

By the way, don't forget to read Stephen King's 'On Writing' first, or every third word will be an adverb. Mine was. 😉

Ross Greenwood, bestselling author of The Detective Inspector Barton series and *The Snow Killer,* which hit the #1 charts at KOBO.

Facebook.com/RossGreenwoodAuthor

BOOK TITLES

NON FICTION

WRITER'S SECRET WEAPON

ROMANTIC SUSPENSE

SMOKE & MIRRORS SERIES

ANXIETY
DUPLICITY
IDENTITY

PARANORMAL ROMANCE

Onyx & Mercury SERIES

A KISS BEFORE DYING
A LONG KISS GOODBYE

SHADES SERIES

DEADLY SHADES #1
SHADES OF HOLLY #2

KILLER SHADES #3
SHADES SERIES BOX SET - BOOKS 1 THROUGH 3

CONTEMPORARY ROMANCE

THE LONG ROAD HOME
PROTECTING KATIE

ABOUT THE AUTHOR

H. D. Thomson moved from Ontario, Canada as a teenager to the heat of Arizona where she graduated from the University of Arizona with a B.S. in Business Administration with a major in accounting. After working in the corporate world as an accountant, H.D. changed her focus to one of her passions—books. She owned and operated an online bookstore for several years and then started the company, Bella Media Management. The company specializes in web sites, video trailers, ebook conversion and promotional resources for authors and small businesses. When she's not enjoying small-town life in Spirit Lake, Iowa or heading her company, she is following her first love—writing.

HDThomson.com